CONCORDE

CONCORDE

STEPHEN SKINNER

MIDLAND

An imprint of
Ian Allan Publishing

Acknowledgements

I would like to take this opportunity to thank the following for the help they have granted me in the compilation and writing of this book.

Pedro Aragao, Barbados Concorde Experience, John Battersby (Bristol Aero Collection), Alan Baxter (Rolls-Royce Historical Trust), Anthony Best, Howard Betts, British Airways Museum, Derek Ferguson, Mike Fielding (BAE SYSTEMS), Carl Ford, Mike Goodall (Brooklands Museum), Barry Guess (BAE SYSTEMS), Phil Jones, Marco Louwe, Vin Man, Mike Phipp, Fabian Rausch, Julie Redfern (Rolls-Royce Historical Trust), Brian Riddle (Librarian, RAeS), Paul Robinson, Pawel Kierzkowski, Captain David Rowland (former BA Concorde Captain), Graham Simons (GMS Enterprises), Frank Skinner, Jean-Pierre Touzeau, Rolando Ugolini, Ben Wang, Rob Ware.

If there is anyone I have overlooked then the oversight is unintentional.

Special thanks

I would also like to thank my wife, Jane, for her continued support, encouragement and editorial contribution.

Author's Note

In a BBC poll in 2006 Concorde was chosen as the greatest design icon of the twentieth century.

Concorde, the world's first and to date only successful supersonic transport entered service in 1976 amid controversy over its cost and warnings over its possible environmental impact, yet became the acme of prestige trans-Atlantic travel. Concorde has been grounded since 2003 yet this iconic aircraft draws the crowds as a museum exhibit where 18 of the 20 built remain as silent witnesses to its achievements in flight, never again to leave the ground at 250 mph and fly at Mach 2 at 60,000 ft.

But Concorde was much more than an icon; it was unique, crossing the Atlantic in half the time of the conventional, dull, plodding airliners. It cruised on the edge of space at 60,000 ft where the sky is a dark blue and the curvature of the earth is evident. It could fly at the speed of a bullet for more than three hours while 100 passengers were transported in luxury, given first-class service by attentive airline cabin staff.

The process of turning the concept of a Supersonic Transport into a fully certified airliner demanded an immense effort from the manufacturers and many other suppliers, Government bodies, and two national airlines, British Airways and Air France. The effort has been compared by some as Britain and France's equivalent to the US Space Programme.

Stephen Skinner
January 2009

Published by Midland Publishing
An imprint of Ian Allan Publishing Ltd, Riverside Business Park, Molesey Road, Hersham, Surrey, KT12 4RG
Printed by Ian Allan Printing Ltd, Riverside Business Park, Molesey Road, Hersham, Surrey, KT12 4RG

Code: 0907/

Visit the Ian Allan Publishing website at
www.ianallanpublishing.co.uk

CONTENTS

FOREWORD

Captain David Rowland, FRAeS FRIN. Former Concorde Pilot and Flight Manager

Captain David Rowland

UNTIL Concorde went into service the only people to go supersonic had had to wear pressure suits and 'bone domes' and were strapped into high performance military aircraft. Even then, in most cases, the supersonic part of the flight lasted for only a few minutes.

Concorde passengers sat in air-conditioned comfort, enjoying a drink and good food, listening to music or reading while they travelled faster than the speed of sound, for two to three hours. Without the speed information displayed in the cabins, they would probably have been unaware of just what an extraordinary experience they were enjoying.

It can be argued that Concorde's real achievement was that it made supersonic flight routine an everyday event for thousands of people.

Throughout its nearly thirty years in service no other aircraft in the world could do what Concorde did; carry 100 people, at twice the speed of sound, across the Atlantic and on other long-haul routes. In the 21st century those achievements might not sound too ambitious, but the origins of the vision that became Concorde lay in the years just after the Second World War, when the jet engine, supersonic flight and the first jet powered passenger aircraft were all very new. When judging Concorde's success, it should be viewed from the perspective of the age of its conception, when crossing the Atlantic took many hours, and possibly several stops, often flying in amongst the clouds and the bad weather.

The journey from vision to in-service operations, more than 20 years later, is a story of achievement of which the United Kingdom and our French colleagues should always be justly proud. The political machinations of the nineteen-sixties, which brought about the threat of cancellation, together with increasing costs and the cancellation of purchase options by the world's airlines as the oil crisis and recession of the nineteen-seventies took hold, should not be allowed to define the Concorde story.

If one of the measures of the success of a project, in engineering terms, is whether the finished product actually achieves the aspirations and challenging specification set out in the original concept, then Concorde must be considered a success.

Concorde was a remarkable aeronautical achievement, and remains unsurpassed even after its retirement from service.

And what about Concorde's performance in service? It was designed to fly between the world's two great financial centres and that's exactly what it did, day in and day out, throughout nearly all of its in-service life and, at least from this side of the channel, it did it successfully, both operationally and commercially. 'Time' was Concorde's commodity. Westbound, it flew across time zones faster

than the sun and therefore, in *local* time, passengers would arrive in New York an hour or so *before* departing from London. Business travellers, for whom time really is money, could leave their home or office in the UK at a sensible hour in the morning and arrive in New York just after breakfast; in time for a full day's work, having crossed the Atlantic to get there. Of course the direction of the earth's rotation made it impossible to achieve the same sort of 'time travel' in an eastbound direction, but the 'red eye' overnight Trans-Atlantic flight to Europe was a thing of the past with Concorde.

On the right routes there were always enough people who would appreciate the benefits of Concorde travel and would pay the premium for it. The Concorde business was good and, for most of its in-service life, profitable for British Airways.

The Concorde story is one of vision, innovation, co-operation and success and this book is a valuable reminder of what it is possible to achieve in aviation, and a pictorial record of that beautiful shape that no longer graces our skies.

Captain David Rowland

January 2009

Biography

Captain David Rowland FRAeS FRIN

David Rowland was born and educated in Sheffield, South Yorkshire. He joined BOAC in 1969 as a co-pilot/navigator on VC 10 aircraft, subsequently joining the Concorde fleet as a co-pilot in 1976, soon after the aircraft entered service.

Having left Concorde to obtain a command on BAC 1-11 aircraft he became a Training Captain and Instrument Rating Examiner. He returned to Concorde as a Captain and Flight Manager of the Fleet, later becoming Concorde Commercial Manager and then Concorde General Manager, bringing together operational and commercial responsibility. He retired from British Airways in 1999.

David is a Fellow of the Royal Aeronautical Society and RAeS President (2008-09). He is a founder committee member of the aviation industry's environmental group, Greener-by-Design and was Chairman of the Operations sub-committee. He is also a Founder Member of the Oxfordshire Branch of the Society.

He is a Fellow of the Royal Institute of Navigation and a Liveryman of the Guild of Air Pilots and Air Navigators.

On 14 October 1947 the rocket-powered Bell X-1 flown by 'Chuck' Yeager was the first aircraft in the world to exceed Mach 1. The Bell X-1 was mounted beneath a Boeing B-29 Superfortress and flown up to 23,000 ft where it was dropped clear of the mother craft. Its rocket motors were then ignited, propelling it to 43,000 feet and a speed of Mach 1.06 (700 mph). In this photograph 'Chuck' Yeager (on the left) is seen with fellow USAF test pilots Gus Lundqvist and Jim Fitzgerald and the Bell X-1 which was named 'Glamorous Glennis' as a tribute to Yeager's wife. (Author's collection)

IN 1939 the German Heinkel He 178 had made the first flight of a jet-powered aircraft and two years later the British Gloster E28/39 powered by a jet engine devised by Sir Frank Whittle took to the air. These designs soon led to wartime jet fighters such as the Germans' swept-wing Messerschmitt Me 262 and the rather more conventional British Gloster Meteor. By the end of the Second World War there was already a number of military jet aircraft nudging the speed of sound, i.e. Mach 1, and when hostilities ceased the Allied powers were glad to benefit from their access to German aircraft research and sought to build aircraft that would be supersonic. The British even had an aircraft, the Miles M.52, in build which would almost certainly have achieved this goal but the project was cancelled before flight and the details of the design passed to the Americans.

As a result the accolade for the first supersonic level flight was achieved in the USA when Chuck Yeager exceeded Mach 1 in level flight in the rocket-propelled Bell X-1 in October 1947 in an aircraft which bore some resemblance to the Miles M.52.

British supersonics

The first British aircraft to exceed Mach 1, the small de Havilland 108 jet flown by John Derry, reached this speed in an uncontrolled steep dive in September 1948. It was not until 5 August 1954 that Britain could equal the American achievement when Roland Beamont took the English Electric P.1A to Mach 1 in level flight on its third flight. In March 1956 the Fairey Delta 2 flown by Peter Twiss set a new world speed record for Britain of 1,132 mph (Mach 1.73). This represented an increase of some 300 mph over the record set in August 1955 by an American

On 9 September 1948, the turbo-jet-powered de Havilland DH108 VW120 flown by John Derry exceeded Mach 1.0 in an uncontrolled vertical dive from 40,000 to 30,000 ft, becoming the first British aircraft to exceed the sound barrier. Three DH108s were built to investigate the behaviour of swept wings for the Comet. As a tailless aircraft it had elevons on the trailing edge of the wing (i.e. combined ailerons and elevators). All three DH108s crashed, killing their pilots. (BAE SYSTEMS)

F-100 Super Sabre. The Fairey Delta 2 thus became the first aircraft to exceed 1,000 mph in level flight.

Efforts continued apace. On 25 November 1958, with Beamont again at the controls, the English Electric P.1B, a development of the P.1A, became the first British aircraft to reach Mach 2.0 in level flight. The P.1B was developed into the Lightning, which became the RAF's Mach 2 fighter in the 1960s.

French research

After its wartime defeat France and its aviation industry had made a remarkable recovery. On 3 August 1954, two days before the English Electric P.1A's supersonic achievement, the delta-winged Nord Gerfaut exceeded Mach 1 in level flight and became the first European aircraft to do so. André Turcat, who later piloted Concorde on its maiden flight, also led much of the test-flying of the Gerfaut and in 1957 broke five time-to-altitude records. Subsequently Turcat took over the Nord 1500 Griffon test programme, one of the world's first ramjet-powered aircraft which he took to Mach 2.19 in 1958. This was part of a series of competing programmes to fulfil a French Air Force specification for a Mach 2 fighter. It featured a dual powerplant, with the turbojet enabling unassisted take-offs and the ramjet producing extra thrust at airspeeds above 600 mph. However, major technical difficulties in developing an operationally reliable ramjet led to the cancellation of the Griffon programme in favour of the Dassault Mirage.

The small delta-winged Mirage 1, powered by two Viper turbojets, flew on 25 June 1955 and demonstrated considerable potential. This led to the much larger Mirage 3 which achieved Mach 2 in level flight on 24 October 1958, just ahead of Beamont and the P.1B. While Britain abandoned the Fairey Delta 2, the similarly-configured Mirage design proved a winner and sold throughout the world. The much larger Mirage 4 served as a nuclear bomber with the French Air Force and was employed as a research aircraft during the Concorde programme.

Yet even as the British and French were exploring supersonic speeds with military jets, thoughts were turning to supersonic airliners – thoughts which were to culminate in Concorde.

Below and right: Just two days after the Gerfaut on 5 August 1954 and on only its third flight, the English Electric P.1 piloted by Roland Beamont exceeded the sound barrier in level flight with 'cold' thrust, i.e. without reheat. (Author's collection)

Left: The Fairey Delta 2 WG774 piloted by Peter Twiss achieved a World Speed Record of 1,132 mph (or Mach 1.73) on 10 March 1956. The aircraft could have gone even faster but was restricted by its limited fuel capacity. Owing to the aircraft's delta wing and high angle of attack when landing, the Fairey Delta 2 was fitted with a droop nose which was incorporated in a similar fashion on Concorde. WG774 was later reconfigured with a lengthened fuselage and a new wing as the BAC 221 to carry out aerodynamic research into Concorde. (Author's collection)

The Dassault Mirage 3 prototype became the first European aircraft to achieve Mach 2 in level flight on 24 October 1958. The Mirage was successfully developed into a fighter and ground attack aircraft by Dassault, making huge export sales. (Author's collection)

On 25 November 1958 English
Electric P.1B prototype XA847
piloted by Roland Beamont became
the first British aircraft to fly at
Mach 2.0. This prototype had first
flown on 4 April 1957, reaching
Mach 1.2 on its first flight.
The P.1B was later named the
Lightning and served with the
RAF, Saudi Arabian Air Force
and the Kuwaiti Air Force.
(Author's collection)

The Nord Griffon was one of the
world's first ramjet-powered aircraft.
André Turcat, who later made the
first flight of Concorde, piloted the
maiden flight of the Griffon on
20 September 1955. He flew the
second Griffon at Mach 2.19 in
October 1959. (Author's collection)

Left: The de Havilland Comet 4C depicted here was the final development of the Comet design which first flew in 1949. The Comet was the world's first jet airliner and was predicted to have a great future but less than two years after entering service it was stricken by fatal crashes caused by metal fatigue. This caused a hiatus in production and although this was later resumed and the Comet was developed, it never reached its expected potential. BOAC's Comet 4s opened the first transatlantic jet services in 1958 but were soon replaced by Boeing 707s. This Comet 4C ST-AAW was delivered to Sudan Airways in 1962. (Author's collection)

Hawker Siddeley Trident 2 G-AVFC, the third of BEA's 15-strong initial Trident 2 fleet. The Trident was very narrowly defined to suit the specification of its initial and major customer, BEA, but this made it unattractive to other customers and it failed to make substantial sales. (BAE SYSTEMS)

AFTER the war Britain initially developed airliners which were heavily influenced by wartime designs. But the industry soon broke out of this mould. Among the larger types produced was the turboprop Vickers Viscount which sold widely throughout the world. The first jet airliner, the de Havilland Comet, also deserved to succeed but failed to achieve great sales success because of metal fatigue which caused a lengthy hiatus in production. Even so, the Comet was the first airliner to operate a transatlantic jet service, although it was eclipsed by the larger Boeing 707.

Other larger airliner types were produced but were not generally successful. The Hawker Siddeley Trident was shrunk to suit British European Airways but was then too small for world markets in which it was massively outsold by the Boeing 727. The VC10, a late entry in

the transatlantic jet market behind the Boeing 707, was built for BOAC. Yet it was virtually rejected by the airline, crippling its sales potential. The short-haul BAC One-Eleven, a jet-powered Viscount replacement, had achieved 60 orders by the time of its first flight in 1963 and seemed to have a bright future. But development was too slow and the One-Eleven too was outsold by its American competitors.

France did not produce any airliners in great quantity until the appearance of the medium-range Sud Aviation Caravelle. It flew for the first time in 1955 under the power of two Rolls-Royce Avon turbojets located at the rear of the aircraft. For the time this was a revolutionary layout but one which proved highly fashionable. The Caravelle proved to be successful and was bought by many airlines including major operators such as Air France, Swissair, SAS, Alitalia, Iberia, Finnair and

Big jet taking off on a short runway. One of the VC10s built for British United Airways taking off from Vickers' factory airfield at Brooklands, Weybridge on its maiden flight. Like the Trident the Vickers VC10 also failed to make much headway in world markets against American competition. British Airway's Super VC10s flew transatlantic routes alongside Concorde in the late 1970s. (BAE SYSTEMS)

United Airlines of the USA. Almost 300 were sold and the Caravelle remained in production until 1973.

Only two years after the world-leading Comet entered service in 1952, British aeronautical engineers at the Royal Aircraft Establishment, Farnborough, began to consider the feasibility of a supersonic airliner. As early as 1955 designers had determined that the most effective shape would be a slender delta. This would offer high-speed capability and good low-speed handling, albeit with the drawback of a high angle of attack on landing.

The Supersonic Transport Aircraft Committee, with representation from both the aircraft and aero-engine industry and the Government, was formed in November 1956 to promote research into supersonic airliners. This committee examined all aspects of supersonic airliner operation and tabled a report ambitiously recommending the go-ahead for two supersonic designs. One would have had a capacity for 150 passengers and transatlantic range at Mach 1.8, while the other would have carried 100 passengers over medium ranges at a speed of Mach 1.2. Most of the companies had instigated studies which were considered by the committee but in March 1959 when its report was submitted only Bristol and Hawker Siddeley were selected to produce feasibility studies for Mach 2.2 and Mach 2.7 airliners respectively. From these studies Bristol, led by its Chief Engineer Archibald Russell, was chosen to develop its design for a 132-seater powered by six Bristol Olympus engines. This evolved into the Type 223, a 100-seat slender delta concept with four Olympus engines. This is recognisable as a progenitor of Concorde.

Meanwhile, Sud Aviation was also investigating a replacement for its successful medium-range Caravelle. It devised a delta-winged medium-range 70-80 seat Mach 2 airliner. Provisionally called the Super Caravelle, it was similar in overall configuration to the Bristol Type 223. Not only was the configuration of both designs similar but both manufacturers had also selected the Olympus as their choice of powerplant. As a result, talks between the British and French companies to explore the possibility of collaboration were held in Paris on 8 June 1961.

Meanwhile, the UK aircraft manufacturing industry had been restructured in 1960. Bristol Aircraft became part of the British Aircraft Corporation (BAC) along with Vickers-Armstrong and English Electric. In 1977 BAC was nationalised together with Hawker Siddeley Aviation to form British Aerospace, later privatised in 1981. The French partner,

Sud Aviation was a nationalised company which had been formed in 1957 by the merger of two smaller state-owned aircraft manufacturers, Sud-Est and Sud-Ouest. In 1970 Sud Aviation merged with Nord Aviation to form Aérospatiale.

Go–ahead

By 1962 the project had become a vital element of the Foreign Office strategy for securing entry to the Common Market, now the European Union. A co-production agreement was seen as an important signal of Britain's pro-European credentials with the project demonstrating the kind of industrial expertise Britain would contribute. Britain and France therefore agreed to co-operate on a joint study into the development and manufacture of a supersonic airliner. Negotiations culminated in the signing on 29 November 1962 of two agreements, one between the French and British Governments, the other between the manufacturers to whom the project was entrusted. The agreements provided for the construction of two Concorde prototypes followed by two pre-production aircraft as well as two airframes for static and fatigue testing. The first flight of the prototype was expected to be in the second half of 1966. Development costs were estimated at between £150 and £170m.

Neither of these targets was met: Concorde did not fly until 1969 and expenditure continued to escalate, regularly causing uproar in the press and providing ammunition for the project's opponents. But despite persistent opposition on both sides the project did go ahead, with the total cost to British and French taxpayers exceeding £2,000m.

Fortunately for Concorde, the treaty signed by the two Governments contained an extraordinary caveat apparently engineered by Julian Amery, Britain's Conservative Minister of Aviation. This stated that if either side withdrew from the agreement it would have to bear all the development costs. The threat of such a heavy financial penalty was to thwart the Labour Government's later efforts to withdraw from the project.

The Anti-Concorde Project

Concorde had to fend off a vociferous anti-lobby led by Richard Wiggs who established the Anti-Concorde Project in 1966. It was financed by money raised from newspaper advertisements featuring densely-printed arguments against the supersonic transport. Among the supporters of this cause were Mary Goldring, aviation correspondent

Left: The five One-Elevens completed at BAC's Hurn factory in December 1967: two for the Royal Australian Air Force A12-125 and A12-124, one for Bavaria Flug D-ANDY, and VASP of Brazil's PP-SRT and PP-SRU. The BAC One-Eleven was designed as a Viscount replacement and soon amassed a strong order book. Though 244 One-Elevens were built, failure to develop it speedily enough led to it being massively outsold by its American competitors.
(BAE SYSTEMS)

The Sud Aviation Caravelle was the only French-built jet airliner prior to Concorde and France's only successful airliner.
It flew in 1955 and served with many of the Europe's major airlines such SAS (Scandinavian Airlines System) whose SE-DAI was photographed at Stockholm – Arlanda in October 1966.
(Lars Söderström)

of *The Economist* and a steadfast opponent of Concorde. She sought every opportunity to highlight the project's cost to the country, citing the aircraft's economics, its noise and environmental impact as reasons to cancel it. Some in the media insisted that ancient monuments would collapse in the wake of the boom. Swedish academic Bo Lundberg claimed Concorde would cause radiation that would result in the world's destruction. Possibly as a result of his dire predictions, Sweden, Norway, West Germany, Holland, Switzerland and the USA prohibited supersonic flights over their territory.

Left: A wind tunnel model of Concorde showing the vortices formed on the leading edge of the wing. Whereas on conventional aircraft vortices are only created at the wing tips, when Concorde flew at a high angle of attack the amount of vortex lift generated by the wing increased significantly enabling it to fly at slow speeds on approach and landing. (BAE SYSTEMS)

WHEN engineers first examined the SST concept in the 1950s they based their experience on military aircraft which could make a short dash at supersonic speed. But a supersonic airliner would need to carry a large number of passengers and maintain supersonic speeds for several hours. This presented a series of huge technical challenges and an exhaustive programme of research, development and testing had to be devised to establish the feasibility of producing a supersonic airliner. The many technically advanced engineering features eventually embodied in Concorde represented the culmination of thousands of hours of ground and flight testing.

Design

Both Bristol and Sud had adopted a similar layout for their respective concepts leading to the distinctive Concorde design. But a huge amount of work was concentrated on refining the design, which was far more critical than that of conventional airliners. The slender delta wing had to generate sufficient lift throughout the speed range. At low speeds it produced vortex lift which made it controllable, albeit with a high angle of attack. The shape was actually very complex with droop and twist along the leading edge with camber and taper across the whole wing. This refinement continued throughout the development process resulting in the third Concorde being longer than the first two prototypes. The fourth was even longer as it had an extended rear fuselage to reduce drag.

Structure

The choice of material for the skin of the aircraft was dictated by the decision to choose a cruising speed of Mach 2. A higher speed would have necessitated stainless steel or titanium. BAC had encountered more than enough trouble in building the BAC 188 out of stainless

steel to want to use it on a supersonic transport. In any case the significant challenge posed by a supersonic airliner would be that of 'creep' expansion of the metals employed as a result of the heat generated by its speed and consequent impact on the structural loads. The temperature at the extreme nose was expected to reach 127 degrees C and 91 degrees C at the tail, causing the aircraft to expand during supersonic cruise. The temperatures on the wing also varied. A copper-based aluminium alloy previously used in gas turbine blades was therefore selected and had to be made in quantity for the new airliner.

To test the structure two static test airframes were constructed. The static test programme at Toulouse on the third airframe built was completed in September 1973. It was tested to destruction in June 1974. The sixth airframe, the fatigue test specimen, was tested at RAE Farnborough and was used to assess durability by simulating the life of the aircraft. The airframe was subjected to repeated 'flights' or cycles which ceased when it reached 20,000. Both specimens were heated and cooled continuously so that the fuselage stresses could represent actual flight. A conservative margin of error was applied so that the aircraft was deemed safe to make 6,700 flights or to operate until 2008.

A diagram indicating the range of temperatures experienced by Concorde during a Mach 2.0 cruise. (BAE SYSTEMS)

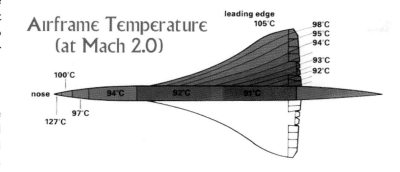

Airframe Temperature (at Mach 2.0)

leading edge 105°C

98°C
95°C
94°C
93°C
92°C

nose

100°C

94°C   92°C   91°C

97°C
127°C

Years later when it was appreciated how profitable Concorde had become, British Airways gave some thought to extending this limit. G-BOAF, the final Concorde built, was fitted with strain gauges and measuring equipment to further examine the life of the aircraft. As a result the manufacturers deemed that Concorde's life could be extended to 8,500 flight cycles or until approximately 2015.

Flying controls

Concorde was the first commercial aircraft to employ 'fly by wire' control technology which has now become the norm for airliners. Traditionally, when the pilot moves the control column or 'stick', the flying controls move via a direct mechanical linkage in a way appropriate to the command. Fly by wire, however, employs electrical signalling between the control column and rudder bar and the hydraulically-actuated flying controls. This control system was duplicated but in the event of the failure of both, a standby mechanical system was still available.

Most airliners use ailerons for lateral control, elevators for longitudinal control and leading edge and trailing edge flaps to increase lift during take-off and landing. But Concorde's wing fulfilled both its high speed and its low speed roles without requiring any moving surfaces other than elevons – combined elevators and ailerons – located on the wing's trailing edge. When Concorde was parked, the elevons would droop because the hydraulic system was not functioning.

The three hydraulic systems also powered the nose visor as well as undercarriage actuation. The twin-wheel nose gear retracted forwards into the nose, while the four-wheel main units retracted sideways into the central section.

Flight simulators at both Filton and Toulouse played an important part in the development programme. This enabled significant investigations to be made into SST flight control systems and handling characteristics well in advance of the first aircraft's completion.

Visor

The anhedral slender delta wing with its ogival leading edge was the result of a huge amount of wind tunnel testing. This configuration resulted in Concorde adopting a high angle of attack which would have made it difficult for the pilots to see the ground on approach and landing. To counteract this the aircraft incorporated a device used on the Fairey Delta 2. As a result, the nose was drooped hydraulically to improve

forward view during take-off, initial climb, approach and landing. A retractable visor was raised hydraulically to provide a smooth aerodynamic shape during cruising flight. The visor on the two prototype Concordes was of solid metal construction with just two small poorly-positioned windows to provide forward vision. Complaints by the test pilots were ignored until the US Federal Aviation Administration indicated that it would decline to certificate the aircraft in such a configuration. A hasty redesign was instigated resulting in a transparent visor which was fitted to the third Concorde onwards.

Systems

Most of Concorde's fuel was stored in the wings. There it not only fuelled the engines and trimmed the aircraft but also acted as coolant

to reduce the temperature of the cabin air, engine fittings and heat-sensitive equipment. Fuel was pumped into trim tanks in the rear fuselage during acceleration and then forwards during deceleration to subsonic speed to counteract rearward shift in the centre of lift as the aircraft went supersonic. This maintained the correct relationship between the centre of gravity and aerodynamic centre of pressure by transferring fuel rearwards during acceleration and forwards during the return to subsonic flight.

Most notable of the test rigs was the massive one at Filton which comprised a movable platform and a complete replica of the aircraft's fuel system. During each test the platform was moved to simulate the

attitude and acceleration the aircraft would experience in flight at the actual fuel temperatures and pressures and rates of climb and descent. Use of this rig enabled modifications to the fuel management system to be introduced early in the programme. Other rigs were constructed to test the hydraulic, electrical and engine air intake system together with the air conditioning and landing gear.

Research aircraft

To support the ground and theoretical research two British aircraft were especially constructed to test the slender delta concept. The Handley Page HP115 was designed to examine the low-speed, high

Right: A test rig was constructed at Filton which was a movable platform with a complete replica of the aircraft's fuel system. During tests the platform moved to simulate the attitudes and accelerations that the aircraft would experience in flight at the actual fuel temperatures and pressures and rates of climb and descent. This rig enabled modifications of the fuel management system to be introduced early in the programme. (BAE SYSTEMS)

A mock-up of the later visor design showing it (from the top) configured for supersonic flight, subsonic flight and approach to landing. (Author's collection)

angle of attack performance of the slender delta wing. It made its maiden flight from RAE Bedford on 17 August 1961 and proved that Concorde would not need complicated high lift devices on its wings.

The second machine was a major modification of the Fairey Delta 2, redesignated as the BAC 221. The aircraft was lengthened and fitted with a new engine and undercarriage. The transformation took more than three years to make and it did not fly until 1 May 1964, only embarking on research flying two years later. The new wing was not

representative of Concorde's as the 221 had been designed to support Hawker Siddeley's supersonic project which had lost out to the BAC 223. The 221, however, proved useful in investigating the low-speed aspects of Concorde flight. Both the HP115 and the BAC221 are preserved at the Fleet Air Arm Museum, Yeovilton, together with the first British Concorde prototype G-BSST.

Cabin layout

Concorde's pilot and co-pilot were seated side-by-side on the narrow flight deck. Facing them were the flight instruments. The engine controls were located in between, the controls for the autopilot on the glare shield and emergency controls on the overhead panel. The throttles were situated on the console between the pilots and within reach of the flight engineer seated behind who had a large panel of instruments for the engines and systems to the right. There was also a supernumerary position or jump seat.

Initially there was a wide variety of passenger seating arrangements to suit the individual requirements of the airlines which had

The Handley Page HP115 XP841 was one of two bespoke research aircraft built to investigate Concorde's flight envelope. It was built with a 75° swept delta wing to explore the low-speed handling regime of the slender delta. The HP115 proved that slender deltas were quite flyable at low speeds. In this view, the HP115 is seen from behind showing its sharply swept-back wing, the pod for the pilot and its rather ungainly fixed undercarriage. It was flown by British and French Concorde test pilots, Brian Trubshaw, John Cochrane, Peter Baker, Gilbert Defer and Jacques Guignard. (BAE SYSTEMS)

The other bespoke research aircraft was the BAC 221 registered WG774, an extensive rebuild of the World Record holder Fairey Delta 2 designed to explore the supersonic and subsonic research into delta planforms. It is seen here taking off at the 1964 Farnborough Air Show. (Bristol Aero Collection)

BAC was responsible for the three forward sections of the fuselage, the rear fuselage and vertical tail surfaces, the engine nacelles and ducting, the electrical system, sound and thermal insulation, oxygen system, fuel system, engine installation and fire warning and extinguishing systems. Sud Aviation was responsible for developing and producing rear cabin section, wings and wing control surfaces, hydraulic systems, flying controls, navigation systems, radio and air conditioning. The automatic flight control system was designed by Marconi in the UK and SFENA in France.

Initially there was a common design available to suit French wishes in a medium-range form and a long-range configuration for the British. The only major difference would be in the fuel tankage and therefore in range and weights. But the airlines showed little interest in the medium-range version and it was dropped in 1963.

Two assembly lines were established, at Bristol and Toulouse, requiring a substantial infrastructure to support the production effort and the movement of airframe sections between sites. This was a costly decision but necessary for political and prestige reasons. Today, although major parts for the Airbus family of aircraft are built throughout Europe, final assembly is centred on one site.

Work was soon in progress following the agreement to go ahead. A large number of committees to manage the project had to be established and daily commuting took place between Filton and Toulouse. Remarkably, it was accepted that both metric and imperial measurements should be employed and both English and French languages were used.

The first metal for Concorde prototypes was cut in April 1965 with sub-assembly starting in October. Final assembly of Concorde 001 commenced at Toulouse in April 1966, followed shortly afterwards by Concorde 002 at Filton in August 1966.

Although the main work-sharing had already been established, the allocation of contracts to approximately 600 British and French suppliers for ancillary equipment did lead to disagreement. There were many squabbles involving all the participants throughout the programme but much was learned from managing this huge collaborative and technical effort which could be incorporated in later international aviation projects.

reserved options. In the end both the carriers which operated Concorde settled for a four-abreast 100-passenger layout with two galley areas. Toilets were situated at the front and centre of the cabin. There was a baggage hold under the forward cabin and in the fuselage aft of the passenger accommodation. There were passenger doors forward of the cabin and amidships on the port side with service doors opposite and emergency exits in the rear half of the cabin on each side.

Work share
Manufacture was shared between the British Aircraft Corporation and Sud Aviation (later Aérospatiale), which would build the airframe, and Bristol Siddeley (later Rolls-Royce) and SNECMA (*Société National d'Etude et de Construction de Moteurs d'Aviation*) which would manufacture the engines. France was granted a larger amount of airframe work as Britain had a greater share of that on the Olympus engines.

Right: Concorde manufacturing was shared between Aérospatiale, British Aircraft Corporation, Rolls-Royce, and SNECMA factories. As Britain had a greater share of the engine work the French factories had a proportionally greater share of the airframe build. (BAE SYSTEMS)

A Mirage 4 in front of preserved Air France Concorde F-BVFC at Toulouse in 2004. The Mach 2 Dassault Mirage 4 bomber was flown by test pilots to give them familiarisation of supersonic flight in delta aircraft. (Jean-Pierre Touzeau)

Right: This photograph of the BAC 221 WG774 (top) and the second Fairey Delta 2 WG777 shows the substantial alterations made to the original Fairey airframe to create the BAC 221. (BAE SYSTEMS)

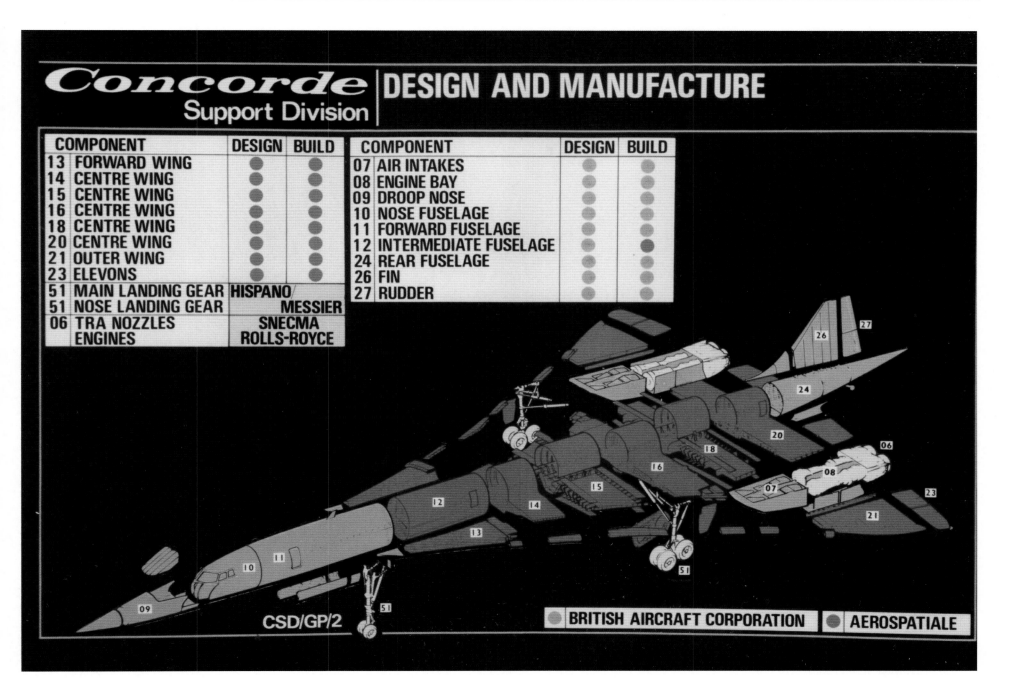

Concorde
Support Division
DESIGN AND MANUFACTURE

COMPONENT	DESIGN	BUILD	COMPONENT	DESIGN	BUILD
13 FORWARD WING	●	●	07 AIR INTAKES	●	●
14 CENTRE WING	●	●	08 ENGINE BAY	●	●
15 CENTRE WING	●	●	09 DROOP NOSE	●	●
16 CENTRE WING	●	●	10 NOSE FUSELAGE	●	●
18 CENTRE WING	●	●	11 FORWARD FUSELAGE	●	●
20 CENTRE WING	●	●	12 INTERMEDIATE FUSELAGE	●	●
21 OUTER WING	●	●	24 REAR FUSELAGE	●	●
23 ELEVONS	●	●	26 FIN	●	●
51 MAIN LANDING GEAR	HISPANO/		27 RUDDER	●	●
51 NOSE LANDING GEAR		MESSIER			
06 TRA NOZZLES		SNECMA			
ENGINES		ROLLS-ROYCE			

CSD/GP/2

● **BRITISH AIRCRAFT CORPORATION**   ● **AEROSPATIALE**

This fuselage mock-up was built at Filton and with its dramatic lighting gave observers their first impression of what Concorde would look like. (Author's collection)

The forward fuselages were built with all flying controls and wiring complete for onward delivery to either the Filton or Toulouse final assembly lines. The amount of complexity involved in the wiring of Concorde is illustrated in this photograph. (BAE SYSTEMS)

The forward fuselage of Concorde 201 registered F-WTSB under construction at BAC's Weybridge factory. (BAE SYSTEMS)

Five forward fuselages being built at BAC Weybridge.
The fuselage nearest to the camera is the first for BOAC
(later British Airways) registered G-BOAC. There are
also two tails on the right. The engineering effort involved
to manufacture these forward fuselages complete with all
systems installed was equivalent to the manufacture of a
complete BAC One-Eleven.
(BAE SYSTEMS)

The tail and fin of Concorde
G-BBDG being constructed at
Weybridge. This Concorde is now
preserved at the Brooklands
Museum on the site of the
Weybridge factory.
(BAE SYSTEMS)

Most parts were delivered by road to
the final assembly sites − here we
see one of the forward fuselages
loaded in a special container about
to leave the Weybridge factory for
either Filton or Toulouse.
(BAE SYSTEMS)

However, some large parts were air-delivered by Super Guppy operated by Airbus. The Super Guppy was a heavily modified version of a Boeing 377 where an entirely new, hugely enlarged fuselage was constructed and a hinged opening nose door fitted to allow for loading. This aircraft, F-BPPA, is now preserved at Toulouse. (Author's collection)

Left: British final assembly took place in the huge Brabazon hangars at BAC Filton, Bristol in which the Brabazon and Britannias had been built. The Concorde nearing completion on the far right is G-BOAC, British Airways' first, and on the far left G-BOAA, British Airways' second aircraft. (BAE SYSTEMS)

Above: French final assembly was centred at Aérospatiale's Toulouse St. Martin factory where the Caravelles were manufactured. The Concorde on the left is pre-production F-WTSA which flew with BA colours on its right side and Air France's on its left. The Concorde on the right is F-WTSB which initially flew in all Air France livery. (BAE SYSTEMS)

Left: English Electric Canberra WD952 was employed as an Olympus test bed and had its 6,500 lbs thrust Rolls-Royce Avons replaced with 9,750 lbs thrust Bristol Olympus engines. The only visible change to the aircraft was the larger nacelles for the Olympuses. Flown by Bristol's Deputy Chief Test Pilot Walter Gibb, it gained the World Altitude Record on 4 May 1953 when it reached 63,668 ft. Specially lightened and re-engined with more powerful Olympuses, it broke the height record again on 29 August 1955 when it reached 65,876 ft. (Bristol Aero Collection)

The logo on the side of the Concorde engine nacelle. It identifies Rolls-Royce and SNECMA as the makers. However the Olympus originated from a Bristol Aero-Engines design of the late 1940s. Bristol Engines became Bristol Siddeley in 1959 and was taken over by Rolls-Royce in 1966. (Author's collection)

THE Olympus engine was of paramount importance to the Concorde project: without it the supersonic transport could not have gone ahead.

Both the British and French concepts leading to Concorde featured the Olympus. A supersonic transport would clearly need an engine with high power for take-off, transonic acceleration and long periods at supersonic speed. Low fuel consumption was a necessity not only for supersonic flight but also when the aircraft passed over land at subsonic speeds. A turbofan would have been less noisy but also too bulky. A low-bypass turbojet was the only choice as it would have a small cross-section and therefore lower drag. Owing to the aircraft's speed the engine also required a complex intake and exhaust system. The Olympus had already shown its potential through its part in setting world altitude records and its performance in the Vulcan bomber.

Viewing a Concorde at a museum the visitor cannot fail to notice the Rolls-Royce and SNECMA logos on the engine nacelles under the wings which acknowledge the British and French companies responsible for the aircraft's propulsion. But the very name, Olympus, indicates the powerplant's actual origin as a product of Bristol Engines, which named its engines after figures from Greek mythology. At that time, incidentally, Rolls-Royce chose to name its products after British rivers. As a result of the rationalisation of the British aircraft industry in 1959, Bristol Engines and Armstrong Siddeley Motors merged to form Bristol Siddeley. In 1966 this company was acquired by Rolls-Royce, leaving only one British aero-engine firm which is now one of only three major manufacturers supplying powerplants for most Airbus and Boeing airliners.

Olympus World Altitude Record

The Olympus originated from a Bristol proposal in 1946 for a long-range bomber for the RAF. Even though the intended recipient never advanced beyond the drawing board, limited development of the engine continued and an early version offering more than 9,000 lbs of thrust ran for the first time in May 1950.

In the late 1940s and `50s when turbojets were still in their infancy it was common for redundant piston-engined wartime aircraft like Lancasters to be employed as engine test beds. But for such a high performance unit as the Olympus a brand-new Canberra (WD952) was delivered to Filton from English Electric's Warton plant to Filton. There its two Rolls-Royce Avon engines were replaced by larger and far more powerful Olympus units. The Canberra was already a sprightly performer with its Avons but the Olympuses gave it double the thrust and its initial rate of climb increased to 15,000 ft per minute. Flights regularly took place at 60,000 ft. This was to be Concorde's cruising altitude and was already above the existing world altitude record.

On 4 May 1953 Bristol's deputy chief test pilot Walter Gibb set out from Filton in a specially-lightened WD952 carrying only the minimum of fuel. By reaching 63,668 ft Gibb gained the record but the flight was not without drama. Both engines flamed out at the peak of the climb and could only be restarted after the aircraft descended to 40,000 ft., enabling it to make a safe return to Filton.

Two years later he did it again. On 29 August 1955 Gibb took off from Filton with even less fuel and the aircraft further lightened. The Olympus-Canberra managed to reach 65,876 ft which was marginally greater than the 3 per cent increase required to validate a new record. Two years' development had ensured that the engines did not cut out this time.

Vulcan

Apart from the first prototype all Avro Vulcans were powered by the Olympus. As the delta-winged bomber was developed different marks of Olympus with greater power were installed, starting at 11,000 lbs of thrust and finally reaching 20,000 lbs. Some Vulcans participated in the engine's development programme as test beds and the power-plant's enduring qualities were to be proved in the twilight of a long RAF career. In 1982 during the Falklands War the Vulcan was thrown into the limelight when it undertook 16-hour bombing sorties from the Ascension Islands to attack the Argentine-held Falkland Islands.

TSR2

While the Vulcan flew at subsonic speeds the next aircraft to be Olympus-powered was required to have Mach 2 performance. In 1959 the RAF issued a requirement for a Canberra replacement and two companies, Vickers-Armstrong and English Electric, won the contract to build it. As a result they merged and, together with Bristol, formed the British Aircraft Corporation which later became Concorde's British builders. It was decided that two 30,610 lb Olympus 320s with reheat would power the aircraft, which was known as the TSR2.

To test fly the TSR2-Olympus 320, Vulcan XA894 was delivered to Filton in July 1960 for the installation of a test engine in a custom-built nacelle on the underside of the aircraft. This gave it a grand total of five Olympuses, the trial unit being mounted under its centre section. XA894 made its maiden flight with a development version of the Olympus 320 in February 1962 and embarked on a test programme.

On 3 December 1962 XA894 was positioned for a full power run of the trial engine on the ground. As it was run

The Olympus-powered BAC TSR2 in its element. Only one example of the TSR2, XR219, flew prior to its cancellation in April 1965. (BAE SYSTEMS)

Following the loss of Vulcan XA894 a replacement aircraft XA903 underwent a lengthy conversion to carry a Concorde Olympus engine in a specimen Concorde nacelle in order to provide accurate information on the engine's performance at subsonic speeds. In this photograph the device below the aircraft's nose and in front of the intake is a water spray rig used to assess performance during icing conditions. (Rolls-Royce Historical Trust)

Concorde

Because both the British and French manufacturers had selected the Olympus for their original supersonic airliner proposals, it was clear that Bristol Siddeley would take the lead on powerplant development. As all Concorde work had to be shared between the two countries the French aero-engine manufacturer SNECMA was chosen to participate. But with a 60:40 division of work it would inevitably be the junior partner and it was given responsibility for the rear end including the reheat system, variable nozzle, noise suppression nozzle, jet pipe and thrust reverser.

The initial version of the powerplant chosen for Concorde was designated as the Olympus 593D. But even before it ran the airliner's design weight rose and a new 593B (B for Big) replaced it. Two 593Ds were built, however, and in September 1964 the engine achieved 29,100 lbs thrust, which was the greatest 'dry' thrust (without reheat or afterburner) ever achieved at the time. The 593B started ground running in November 1965 and by October the following year had run at 35,190 lbs thrust with reheat. One of the other 'bench' engines was run continuously for 505 hours. The first test bed run of the Olympus 593 and variable geometry exhaust assembly was completed at SNECMA's Melun-Villaroche facility in France in June 1966.

As with the TSR2-Olympus a Vulcan was selected to trial the Olympus 593 and its sophisticated intake using a nacelle similar to that destined for Concorde. In that application the Olympuses were mounted in twin nacelles under each wing but on the Vulcan test bed a specialist half-nacelle was fabricated and positioned below the bomb bay. Following a lengthy installation XA903 flew at Filton on 9 September 1966. This was the first occasion on which the Olympus 593 had been aloft and was well ahead of Concorde's maiden flight.

The Vulcan test bed proved an invaluable tool, recording 20,000 items of data per two hour flight. It trialled all aspects of the intake's functioning, the engine's subsonic operation and especially its performance in icing conditions. The intake was of critical importance to Concorde. To function at its optimum the air intake needed to be supplied with air travelling at Mach 0.5, half the speed of sound irrespective of whether or not the aircraft was flying supersonically at high altitude or much more slowly at low level. Computer-controlled variable-area air intakes were therefore required to ensure that each engine received an optimum air flow under all flight conditions.

up to full power there was a flash of light and an explosion. The crew swiftly exited the Vulcan as fuel poured out on to the tarmac and ignited. The fire even spread to a new fire engine which had been positioned to provide cover for the test. The Vulcan then burned for several hours, generating a huge pall of dense black smoke which rose high above Bristol. The incident had been caused by a low pressure turbine disc which had shot out of the engine, travelled around the Vulcan's bomb bay and punctured the fuel tanks. It had then hit the ground, sending shrapnel through the wing fuel tank before careering across the airfield.

From then until the maiden flight of the TSR2 at Boscombe Down in September 1964 all Olympus 320 testing was ground-based. There were still problems with the Olympus 320 but the TSR2 was to make only 24 flights before its cancellation by the Government and the cessation of all flying.

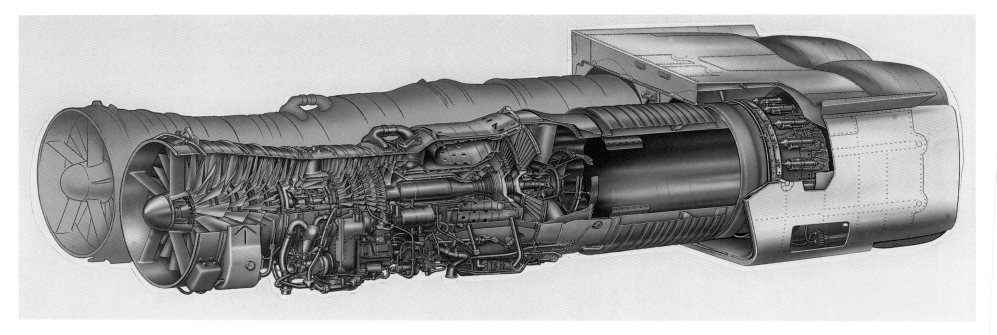

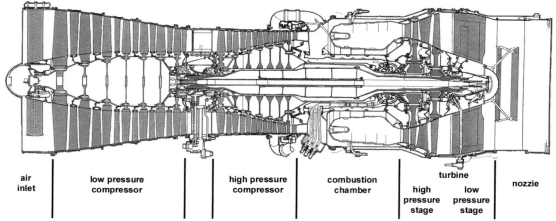

air inlet	low pressure compressor	high pressure compressor	combustion chamber	turbine high pressure stage	low pressure stage	nozzie

During supersonic cruise the Olympus had to swallow air at 101 lbs per sq in at 127 degrees C, which meant that the engines had to be manufactured from titanium and nickel alloys. Likewise, the fuel became hot so the engine had to be tested to ensure it could cope with high temperatures.

Following the maiden flight of Concorde and the gradual raising of the speed envelope, experience was gained in the operation of the engine and its intake at supersonic speeds. A number of Concordes suffered from surging when the flow through the engine was disturbed. In January 1971 the French prototype 001 was decelerating when heavy surging resulted in one of the engines ingesting part of the intake ramp. Remarkably, the engine was then run up to 90 per cent power after the incident. Throughout the trials there was a continuing effort to eradicate exhaust smoke, reduce noise, improve fuel consumption and increase thrust.

Reheat is often employed on supersonic military aircraft to provide a large burst of thrust at take-off and when accelerating to supersonic

An air-brushed illustration showing the twin Olympus installation with reheat jet pipe and thrust reverser assembly as flown on the third and all subsequent Concordes. (BAE SYSTEMS)

Left: A cut-away diagram of an Olympus without the reheat jet pipe. (Rolls-Royce Historical Trust)

A dusk ground test of a Concorde Olympus using reheat, made for a spectacular sight and undoubtedly sound! (Rolls-Royce Historical Trust)

speed. Apart from the unsuccessful Tu-144, Concorde was the only airliner to use it. Reheat involves injecting fuel into the engine exhaust to provide an additional 6,000 lbs thrust. The downside, though, is that it burns a lot of fuel and is extremely noisy. Concorde's reheat was only required for take-off and transonic acceleration and not for the whole flight.

The first Olympus ran at approximately 9,000 lbs thrust in 1950 and its output grew fourfold to more than 38,000 lbs in the final 593

development. When Concorde operations ceased in 2003 the 53-year life of the Olympus appeared to be at an end too. But the veteran Vulcan, owned by the Vulcan to the Skies Trust, flew once more in October 2007 and rejoined the air show circuit.

A CONVENTIONAL airliner requires about 1,000 to 1,500 hours of flight testing before it enters service. But Concorde's revolutionary technology meant that the SST needed more than 5,000 hours. Eight aircraft were involved in the flight test programme which lasted almost seven years. Of this total there were nearly 1,000 hours of route-proving in typical airline service conditions.

Production Concordes were appreciably different from the prototypes and although this resulted in an extension of testing, the actual duration and extent of the programme was not caused by any major difficulty.

Test programme

The programme required the testing of all systems and functionality in all aspects of the aircraft's flight envelope: its entire speed,

attitude and altitude range. Regular and sometimes lengthy groundings occurred from the first flight onwards. This was necessary, for instance, for the installation of updated engines, intakes and control systems.

The Directors of Flight Test of BAC and Aérospatiale, Brian Trubshaw and André Turcat, under the wing of F-WTSS. Trubshaw took part in the taxi trials of F-WTSS prior to its first flight. (BAE SYSTEMS)

Right: Concorde prototype F-WTSS airborne from Toulouse piloted by André Turcat on one of its early flights with British-built Armstrong Whitworth Meteor NF11 acting as a chase aircraft. (BAE SYSTEMS)

F-WTSS positioned to carry out engine runs at Toulouse. The blanketing on the fin was to protect it from acoustic damage and was removed before flight. Note the nose visor lowered to 17½°; this degree of declination was reduced to 12½° as it was found to be unnecessary. (BAE SYSTEMS)

A fine photograph of the French prototype F-WTSS just airborne. This prototype is preserved at the Musée de l'Air, Le Bourget, Paris. (BAE SYSTEMS)

The second British-assembled prototype G-BSST outside the Brabazon hangar at Filton just three days prior to its first flight. (Author's collection)

Flashback to 19 years earlier and the huge Bristol Brabazon in February 1950 parked outside the Brabazon Hangar, which was built for it. Only one Brabazon was completed and never entered production as it was overtaken by technological advances. (Author's collection)

Flashback to 19 years earlier and the huge Bristol Brabazon in February 1950 parked outside the Brabazon Hangar, which was built for it. Only one Brabazon was completed and never entered production as it was overtaken by technological advances. (Author's collection)

BRABAZON Mk.I PROTOTYPE
CENTAURUS 20
FEBRUARY 1950

The programme demanded the testing of the air conditioning and pressurisation, automatic flight control system, avionics, droop nose and visor, electrics, engines and air intakes, flying controls, fuel, icing, internal and external noise, handling, hydraulics, structure, undercarriage and brakes as well as actual performance. Under these headings there were many additional items together with the requirement to assess simulated failures and the support provided by standby systems.

The first four Concordes were solely intended for flight testing. Accordingly, they carried approximately 12 tons of on-board electronic test instrumentation which could record 3,000 different parameters on magnetic tape for analysis on the ground. In addition, basic flight information was continuously relayed by telemetry to a ground monitoring centre. The test equipment itself had to be tested, regularly modified and calibrated.

Flight Test Centres

The French had an excellent production and test centre at Toulouse. Extensively developed for Concorde, it is much in demand today for Airbus work. But the British production team was not so fortunate. Director of flight test, Brian Trubshaw, insisted that the runway at Filton was insufficiently long and not level enough, resulting in the establishment of a test centre at nearby Fairford. This remained in operation until the main part of the test programme ended in November 1976 when it was closed and operations transferred to Filton. Having joint test centres – and production lines – was an unnecessary extravagance but one which proved politically impossible to overcome.

The first two Concorde prototypes

The first two Concorde prototypes were very different from the final aircraft. Shorter and lighter, they were each fitted with a metal visor over the front cockpit windows which severely restricted vision and was raised for supersonic flight. When test and airline pilots and the FAA said it was totally unsuitable the visor was replaced by a much improved and fully glazed design which was installed on subsequent aircraft.

Ceremonial Roll-out

The first prototype, registered F-WTSS (TSS for *Transport Supersonique*) was rolled out at Toulouse on 11 December 1967 to great acclaim. About 1,100 VIPs and other guests had to endure the

British Concorde prototype G-BSST just airborne on its maiden flight from Filton to Fairford on 9 April 1969. (Author's collection)

Three Flight Test Observers on Concorde G-BSST wearing pressure helmets and suits, life jackets and parachutes in the event of the need to use the emergency escape hatch at altitude. Note the amount of test equipment fitted in the cabin. (BAE SYSTEMS)

Tony Benn conceded the French spelling, remarking that 'e' stood 'for excellence, England, Europe and entente.'

Maiden flight and trials of F-WTSS

001 made its first taxi trials on 20 August 1968 with André Turcat and Brian Trubshaw, the French and British directors of flight operations, at the controls. But there were many more aspects to be checked before the aircraft took to the air seven months later. On Saturday 2 March 1969 001 made a 42-minute maiden flight from Toulouse with an all-French crew comprising pilots André Turcat and Jacques Guignard, flight engineer Michel Rétif and flight test engineer Henri Perrier.

The first flight pilots of G-BSST, British Aircraft Corporation Director of Flight Test Brian Trubshaw (left) and John Cochrane on the flight deck of G-BSST. (BAE SYSTEMS)

cold while listening to speeches by politicians including Britain's Minister of Technology, Tony Benn. The French President Charles de Gaulle had already proposed the name 'Concorde' when referring to the Anglo-French supersonic aircraft in January 1963. BAC had agreed to this name, spelling it with the final 'e' from an early stage. The British Government had refused to follow suit but in his speech at Toulouse

Britain's other Concorde? Actually the Cunliffe-Owen Concordia, a 10-seat medium-range transport designed and built at Eastleigh, Hampshire in 1947. Only two were built as the aircraft could not compete with the many surplus DC-3s available post-war and the firm went out of business. (Author's collection)

Interspersed with regular spells on the ground for the installation of new equipment, 001 gradually explored Concorde's flight envelope. It reached Mach 1.05 on 1 October 1969 and Mach 2 on 4 November. Almost every flight by 001 and the British prototype 002 during this period established new achievements for Concorde.

On 23 January 1971 001 suffered a severe incident when reheat was cut on one of the engines at Mach 1.98. The engine surged, causing the adjacent one to follow suit. These surges led to a failure of the intake and pieces of it being ingested by the engines. A safe return was made to Toulouse on three engines and modifications were put in hand to prevent a recurrence. On 7 May 1971, while the test programme was still in progress, French President Georges Pompidou became the first head of state to fly supersonically aboard 001.

Having made more than 100 supersonic flights, F-WTSS had now undertaken the majority of its testing tasks and could now be employed on sales tours. That September the aircraft undertook a trouble-free 14-day tour to Brazil and Argentina. F-WTSS then embarked on high incidence tests and automatic landing trials which culminated in its 397th and last flight, to Le Bourget on 19 October 1973 for preservation at the *Musée de l'Air*.

Maiden flight and trials of G-BSST

In contrast to the grandeur and razzmatazz of F-WTSS's roll-out, that of the British prototype 002, G-BSST, at Filton nine months later on 19 September 1968 was a much quieter affair. Only members of the workforce were there to watch it, providing a sharp contrast to the equivalent French ceremony for which the workforce had been sent home. This lack of ceremony evidently annoyed Tony Benn. Despite being the responsible minister and a Bristol MP he had not been invited.

But there were huge crowds present to watch 002 make a 22-minute 50-mile maiden flight from Filton to Fairford on 9 April 1969. On board were pilots Brian Trubshaw and John Cochrane, assisted by

The two prototypes together at Fairford, F-WTSS seen under the tail of G-BSST. The first three aircraft had short tails and were fitted with tail bumpers which extended for take-off and landing. Subsequent aircraft had longer tails and retractable tail wheels. (BAE SYSTEMS)

flight engineer Brian Watts and flight test observers John Allan, Mike Addley and Peter Holding. G-BSST's first flight was not without its problems. First a light aircraft strayed into the aircraft's path but then, critically, on approach to Fairford, both the radio altimeters failed and Trubshaw had to judge the landing by eye. This was a challenging task as the pilot's eyes were 38 ft above the ground.

Only two months after 002's first flight both prototypes appeared in the air together at the Paris Air Show. A few days later 002 flew over Buckingham Palace to help celebrate the Queen's Birthday.

The aircraft flew at Mach 1 for the first time on 25 March 1970. In September it made daily flying appearances at the SBAC's Farnborough Air Show. On the last day, however, bad weather prevented its return to Fairford and the aircraft had to land at London's Heathrow Airport. It was Concorde's first visit there and, although the noise generated on approach drew many complaints, its departure the following day registered little protest. On 4 November 1970 002 was scheduled to fly at Mach 2 just ahead of F-WTSS on the same day. But at Mach 1.35 a fire warning indication caused a return to Fairford, leaving the French prototype to achieve the accolade of being the first to fly at twice the speed of sound. 002 reached Mach 2 on 12 November. But when the right-hand Olympuses were gently throttled back both started surging, generating a huge amount of noise. Developing the intakes' functioning to obviate surging was to be one of the great triumphs of the test programme. By June 1971 the two Concordes had already reached 500 hours in the air while Olympus engine testing totalled 10,000 hours.

Not all of 002's time was spent on testing. It was clearly important for the manufacturers to demonstrate the safety of the aircraft and on 12 January 1972 the Duke of Edinburgh piloted 002 during a two-hour supersonic flight. British Prime Minister Edward Heath followed in May 1973.

On 2 June 1972 G-BSST left Fairford for an elaborate and expensive 45,000-mile, 30-day sales tour of the Far East and Australia. Support was provided by an RAF Shorts Belfast, which carried a spare engine, and a VC10 with engineers and marketing staff on board. Having introduced Concorde to 14 airports in 12 countries, the aircraft returned to Heathrow on 1 July after a trial of serviceability to which the aircraft had stood up well.

But during a demonstration flight at the Weston-super-Mare Air Show on 26 August 1975 the aircraft suffered a failure in its left main undercarriage when the locking stay became disconnected. G-BSST returned to Fairford where a gentle landing by John Cochrane ensured its safe arrival. The landing gear leg was replaced and on 4 March 1976 G-BSST made its final flight to the Fleet Air Arm Museum at Yeovilton. The flight deck crew was the same as that on its first flight.

The pre-production prototypes

Following on from the two prototypes were two pre-production aircraft, numbered 101, registered G-AXDN, and 102, F-WTSA, which were more representative of the final production machines. There were considerable differences, not only between each of the two aircraft but also between them and the prototypes. As a result much of the flight testing had to be repeated.

The third Concorde, G-AXDN, was rolled out at Filton on 20 September 1971 to begin ground testing. It followed the first two prototypes into the air on 17 December 1971, more than a year and a half after G-BSST's maiden flight. As with 002, it was delivered by Brian Trubshaw and John Cochrane from Filton to nearby Fairford. 'XDN was noticeably larger than its predecessors having a forward fuselage longer by 8 ft 6 in. The much-improved fully-glazed visor gave the crew an excellent view at supersonic speed. Less than two months later, on 12 February 1972, it exceeded Mach 1 for the first time.

G-AXDN's main areas of trials activity were the flutter tests required by its longer fuselage as well as supersonic performance and air intake trials. Operating from Tangier it reached the highest speed ever recorded by a Concorde: Mach 2.23 (1,480 mph) at a then record height of 63,700 ft. The final major test tasks were icing trials undertaken at Moses Lake, Washington State, USA for which it was fitted with an external camera and large areas of black markings on the left wing to indicate ice accretion. Icing trials also took place in the UK with 'XDN trailing Boscombe Down's Canberra tanker.

G-AXDN's final flight was on 20 August 1977 when it was delivered from Filton to the Imperial War Museum, Duxford. In command once again were Trubshaw and Cochrane. Just a few days later the runway was shortened by construction of the M11 motorway, which would have prevented airborne delivery.

F-WTSA was even longer than G-AXDN. It had an extended tail designed to reduce drag and was powered by production standard Olympus engines. It first flew from Toulouse, almost a year after

The staff at the BAC Flight Test Centre at Fairford in front of G-BSST. First row, Directors of Flight Test with Trubshaw in the middle; second row, Aircrew and Administrators; third row, Hangar staff; fourth row, Airfield, Housekeeping and Design; back row, Fire, Security, Administrative support and RAF. (BAE SYSTEMS)

RAF fire crew   Flight test department personnel produce the flight programmes, operate the computer, analyse results, prepare reports. RAF support personnel look after air traffic control.   Security officers

Airfield housekeeping staff, drivers, caterers, storemen, secretaries, receptionists.   Design support team look after modifications and minor changes in aircraft design.   Department of Trade and Industry reps   Press officer

men in the hangar. Inspectors examine and clear the aircraft for flight. Technical management; technicians, including electricians and fitters.

Flight test administrative staff. Aircrew including flight test observers, flight engineers and navigators.   Flight operations responsible for communications with Concorde during tests; flight safety equipment team.

J. Cochrane   Brian Trubshaw   R. M. McKinlay
Assistant director flight operations   Director flight test   Assistant director flight test

G-AXDN, on 10 January 1973. It then enjoyed the distinction of making the first Concorde landing in the USA during the inauguration of Dallas, Fort Worth Airport on 20 August 1973. It had flown there via Caracas and returned to Paris by way of Washington. Following certification tests it returned to the USA at the end of January 1974 and flew to Fairbanks, Alaska for cold 'soak' trials to check the performance of the systems at continuous low temperatures. Later the majority of its test work entailed engine development and taxiing and braking tests on wet and dry runways. F-WTSA made its final flight on 20 May 1976 from Toulouse to Paris Orly. It is there now, preserved at the *Musée Delta*.

Production prototypes

G-AXDN and F-WTSA were the first aircraft to be built to approximately final production standard. But even they differed from the aircraft which eventually entered service although they never did so themselves. These were the Concordes which were to bear the brunt of the certification work.

The first production Concorde 201, F-WTSB, first flew at Toulouse on 6 December 1973, reaching Mach 1.57 (a Concorde first) and Mach 2.05 on its second flight. The aircraft concentrated on systems development and certification flying for performance, handling and systems. For much of this time the aircraft was based at Casablanca, Morocco. It remained in regular use for testing until 1982 when it was placed in storage at Charteauroux. It was ferried back to Toulouse on 19 April 1985 for preservation. That was its last flight.

On 13 February 1974 Concorde 202 G-BBDG made a 1 hr 45 mins maiden flight from Filton to Fairford piloted by Brian Trubshaw, reaching a top speed of Mach 1.4. Just over two weeks later 202 visited Toulouse and reached Mach 2 on its 15th flight. It then embarked on intensive tests of systems and handling throughout the entire flight envelope. On 17 August it became the first aircraft to carry 100 passengers at Mach 2 but G-BBDG was to spend much of its time on performance measurement trials, being based at Casablanca and Madrid.

After Concorde had entered airline service there were further trials flown by 202 in 1977 and 1978 at Casablanca to check several modifications. These included thinner intake lips, extended control surfaces and a sharper fin leading edge. The results were improved performance and reduced fuel consumption resulting in increased payload. G-BBDG made its final flight on 24 December 1981 when it was captained by Trubshaw's successor as BAe chief test pilot, Roy Radford.

The final phase of 'DG's career began in April 1984 when it was acquired by British Airways for use as a major source of spare parts. During May 1988, with its tail fin removed, 'DG was moved into a purpose-built hangar at Filton. Following damage to G-BOAF's nose, 'DG's was exchanged for it. In November and December 2002 the aircraft was temporarily positioned in the Brabazon Hangar to allow the fitting and testing of a strengthened cockpit door as required for the Concorde fleets following the 11 September 2001 terrorist attacks in the USA.

With Concorde's withdrawal from service on 30 October 2003 British Airways offered G-BBDG to the Brooklands Museum. It was dismantled between March and May 2004 and transported to Brooklands where it was reassembled. Painted in BA's 1970's livery, it was placed on public display in July 2006.

The manufacturers' development and test-flying programme involved 2,930 flights totalling 6,560 hours including 2,450 hours at supersonic speeds.

Production aircraft

The first Concordes destined for Air France and British Airways, F-WTSC (later F-BTSC) and G-BOAC, flew in January and February 1975 respectively. Following the award of a special-category Certificate of Airworthiness by the French and British authorities, the aircraft then engaged in endurance flights covering more than 700,000 miles between May and September 1975. G-BOAC flew four North Atlantic crossings in one day, 1 September 1975.

Special-category Certificates of Airworthiness were granted in May and June 1975 by the French SGAC and British Civil Aviation Authority, anticipating the full airworthiness certificates which were granted on 13 October and 5 December 1975 respectively. The second pair of production Concordes, F-BVFA and G-BOAA, flew in late 1975 and the next four production aircraft, F-BVFB, G-BOAB, F-BVFC and G-BOAD, were delivered – two each – to Air France and British Airways in 1976. Each received another aircraft, registered F-BVFD and G-BOAE, in 1977. By this time both carriers had the full complement of their original orders.

There were no customers for the remaining four aircraft in production as well as F-BTSC which was already flying. Three Concordes made their maiden flights in 1978: F-WJAM (later F-BTSD), G-BFKW (later G-BOAG) and F-WJAN (later F-BVFF). The final example, G-BFKW (later G-BOAF), first flew from Filton on 20 May 1979. These aircraft remained in limbo until 1980 when they were delivered to Air France and British Airways. Each airline therefore had a fleet of seven Concordes.

Above: On 6 January 1972 the first French prototype F-WTSS joined the two British-assembled Concordes, G-BSST and G-AXDN, at the BAC Flight Test Centre at Fairford. The two prototypes F-WTSS and G-BSST are on the outside of the trio with the initial solid visor and in the middle is G-AXDN with the production model glazed visor. G-AXDN, assembled at Filton, was the first pre-production aircraft and first flew on 17 December 1971. (BAE SYSTEMS)

G-AXDN landing at the 1974 Farnborough Air Show. The black markings on the wing are for ice measurement. G-AXDN is now preserved at the Imperial War Museum, Duxford. (BAE SYSTEMS)

BAC Test pilot John Cochrane commanded 'XDN on 8 April 1974 when it reached Concorde's highest speed of Mach 2.23 and maximum altitude of 63,700 ft. The markings on the side of G-AXDN's flight deck commemorate its Mach 2.23 speed record. (Author's collection)

Concorde G-AXDN filmed during icing trials from Boscombe Down's Canberra WV787 on 13 September 1974. The Canberra was specially modified to spray fine particles of water to produce icing and so the amount of ice accretion on Concorde could then be measured. (Crown Copyright)

The first French-assembled pre-production Concorde F-WTSA. This was the fourth Concorde built and the first to be completed to full Concorde dimensions with the lengthened tail which reduced drag. (BAE SYSTEMS)

Pre-production prototype F-WTSA was based at Fairbanks, Alaska during icing trials in February 1974. (BAE SYSTEMS)

F-WTSA at the opening of Montreal's new International Airport, Mirabel on 4 October 1975; it had flown from Paris to Montreal, via London and Ottawa. Although the subsonic Air Canada Boeing 747 is of interest to some, far more traipse across the apron to have a closer look at the supersonic Concorde.
(BAE SYSTEMS)

The third British Concorde G-BBDG was also part of the development fleet. It first flew from Filton on 13 February 1974 and wore BA livery. 'DG and its French sister F-WTSB were the first Concordes built to virtual production standard. (BAE SYSTEMS)

The flight deck of G-BBDG was very similar to the production standard and very different to that of the first two prototypes. (BAE SYSTEMS)

Far right: The first Concorde for British Airways, G-BOAC, at Melbourne's Tullamarine Airport during route-proving trials prior to certification in August 1975. (BAE SYSTEMS)

Right: Sir George Edwards, Chairman of the British Air Corporation, holding a copy of the British Certificate of Airworthiness of Concorde which permitted it to enter passenger service. Sir George Edwards became Chief Designer of Vickers-Armstrong in 1945 and later Managing Director, eventually retiring from the British Aircraft Corporation as Chairman. Earlier projects under his direction had included the Viking, Viscount, Valiant, Vanguard, VC10, BAC One-Eleven and TSR2. (BAE SYSTEMS)

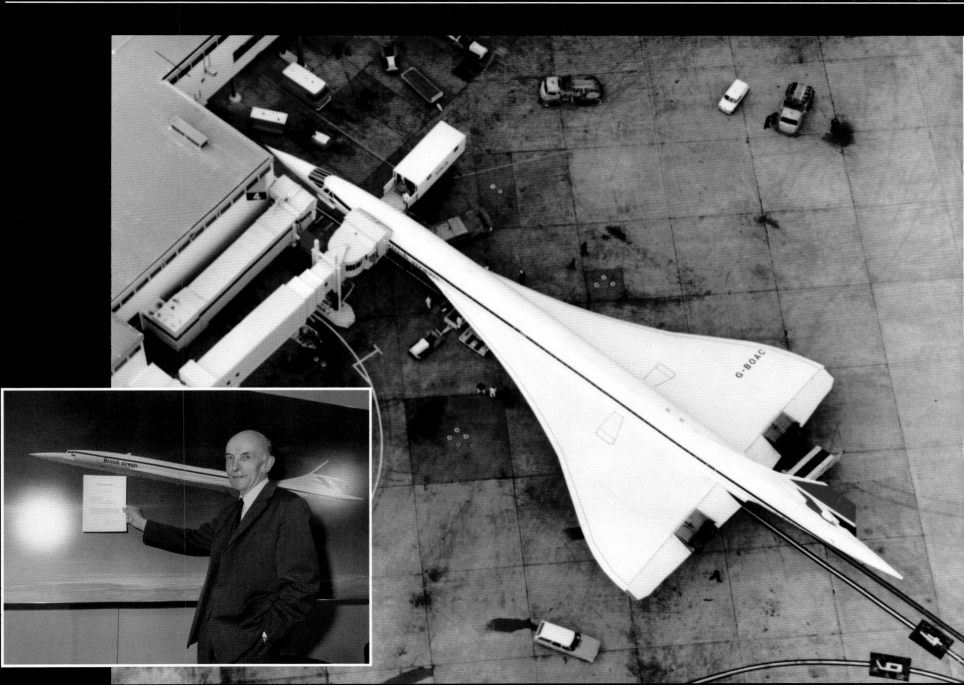

6 · THE BATTLE TO WIN SALES

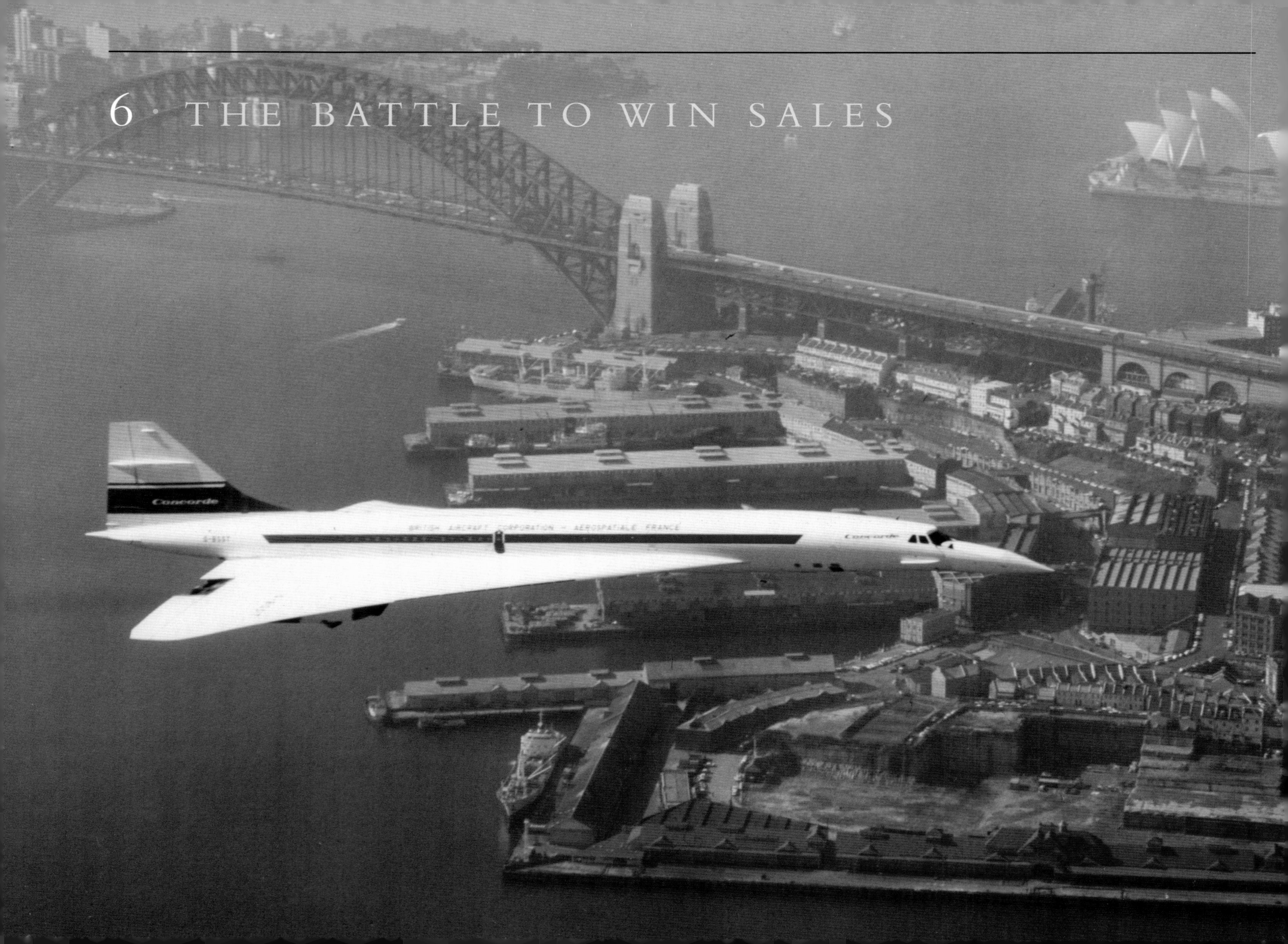

IN the early years of the Concorde project there were forecasts of substantial sales. The US Federal Aviation Administration, for example, thought there would be a market for over 200 SSTs.

Although the initial assumption was that overland supersonic flights would be permissible, this was soon recognised as unrealistic. Since the US covers a vast area, banning overland flight would severely limit route availability and have a damaging effect on the potential market. The sales team's hopes remained high, however, as speed has always sold. It was thought that when passengers were given the opportunity to cut the flying time to Australia from 24 to 15 hours they would be willing to pay a premium. Likewise, halving the time to cross the Atlantic would prove a great boon to many and there would have been similar time savings on other routes.

The first order was an option on six Concordes placed in 1963. This did not come from the state-owned airlines of the two partner countries but from Pan Am, which until its financial collapse in 1991 was the United States' premier international airline and something of a trendsetter within the industry. The two state-owned carriers, British Overseas Airways Corporation and Air France, soon followed suit. By 1967, two years before the first flight, prospects for Concorde were buoyant with 74 options from 16 airlines and potential for substantial further sales. In addition to Pan Am, BOAC and Air France orders had come from Air Canada, American Airlines, Braniff International, Continental, Eastern, TWA and United Airlines in North America, as well as Air India, Japan Airlines, Lufthansa, Middle East Airlines, Qantas and Sabena. In 1972 CAAC of China and Iranair joined in to take the total number of options to 79. The deposits accompanying these options were totally refundable and the contracts would only become firm when guaranteed performance figures had been established by the flight test programme.

In July 1972 British Airways and Air France placed firm orders for five and four aircraft respectively. In the event they were the only two airlines ever to own Concordes. The global oil crisis and the resulting financial insecurity among the airlines unsettled the market for aircraft. On 31 January 1973 Pan Am cancelled its options, followed within hours by TWA. As the crisis deepened during the year the other airlines' options withered away. The option scheme was abandoned and the remaining deposits were refunded. Despite fears that this

When the first orders were placed for Concorde there were two British state-owned airlines, BOAC (British Overseas Airways Corporation) and BEA (British European Airways). These were merged in 1976 to form British Airways, so the first BA Concorde order was under the auspices of BOAC. This is how Concorde would have appeared in BOAC livery with its golden 'Speedbird' (Rolando Ugolini)

Pan American World Airways (Pan Am) was regarded in the 1960s and 1970s as the USA's premier airline and was one of the first three airlines to order Concorde along with British Airways (then BOAC) and Air France. The cancellation of Pan Am's Concorde options in January 1973 was a major blow to the supersonic airliner. This is how it would have appeared in Pan Am's colours. (Rolando Ugolini)

The Paris Air Show mock-up, now in TWA livery. This was the sole occasion when Concorde ever appeared in the livery of an American airline. (Author's collection)

The first French prototype demonstrating at the 1969 Paris Air Show. F-WTSS carried out the first Concorde sales tour when it flew to the Cape Verde Islands, Rio de Janeiro, Cayenne and Sao Paulo in September 1971. (BAE SYSTEMS)

would lead to calls for the project's cancellation, the French and British Governments in July sanctioned the manufacture of 16 production standard Concordes.

As no further orders were received beyond those of BA and Air France, two British and three French-built machines remained unsold. Great efforts were made to sell them and an attempt was made to lease one to Singapore Airlines, although this resulted instead in a joint BA-Singapore Airlines operation in 1979-80. Federal Express seriously considered leasing three Concordes as express parcels carriers but this too came to nothing. Eventually, in September 1979, the sales campaign came to an end with a joint governmental announcement that the remaining two British aircraft were to be delivered to BA with the three unsold French machines going to Air France. This seemed a rather sad end to the manufacturers' original expectations of producing 150 aircraft with a peak output of three aircraft per month.

On 19 October 1976 Concorde F-BTSC departed Charles de Gaulle Airport, Paris on the start of an Asian sales tour. The tour covered 31,000 miles visiting Bahrain, Singapore, Manila, Hong Kong, Djakarta, Seoul and London before returning to Paris. Here F-BTSC is seen at Manila on 5 November 1976 with Imelda Marcos, the wife of the President, boarding to be flown on a shopping visit to Hong Kong. The flight only took one hour as there were no supersonic restrictions. (BAE SYSTEMS)

F-BTSC leaving Heathrow on the final leg of its Asian tour to Paris. It was painted in Air France livery but without Air France titling. During the tour it logged more than 22 hours of supersonic flight out of 32 hours airborne. (BAE SYSTEMS)

Concorde B and beyond

Production did not progress beyond the 16 production aircraft. Subsequent Concordes from aircraft number 17 onwards would have possessed substantially better performance. This would have resulted from an extended full-span wing leading edge droop, extended wing tips and increased fuel tankage. In addition appreciable engine improvements would have meant:

- Quieter take-offs
- Greater range – enabling e.g. Frankfurt–New York non-stop
- Improved fuel consumption

If production had gone into hundreds and the typical aircraft development model had been followed there would have been further improvement beyond the Concorde B specification. This would have offered even greater payload and range.

The final Concorde built, G-BFKX, taking off on its maiden flight from Filton on 20 April 1979. It was painted all white, just like its British-built predecessor, G-BFKW (later G-BOAG), as neither aircraft then had customers and strenuous efforts were made to sell all five unsold Concordes to airlines. When this proved fruitless Air France received the three French examples and BA the British two. When G-BFKX was later delivered to BA it became G-BOAF and is now preserved at Filton. (BAE SYSTEMS)

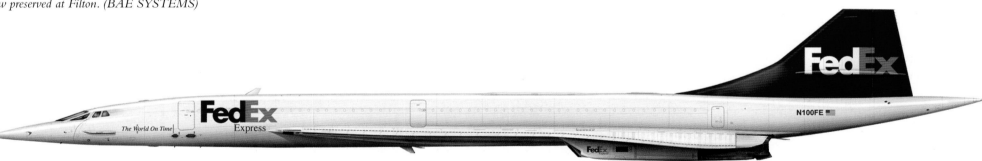

In 1981-82 Federal Express entered negotiations with the manufacturers and the Governments to lease up to three BA Concordes which would have been used for the transport of freight. Unfortunately no agreement was reached for this interesting proposal and Concorde never wore the FedEx livery. (Rolando Ugolini)

7 · US AND SOVIET COMPETITION

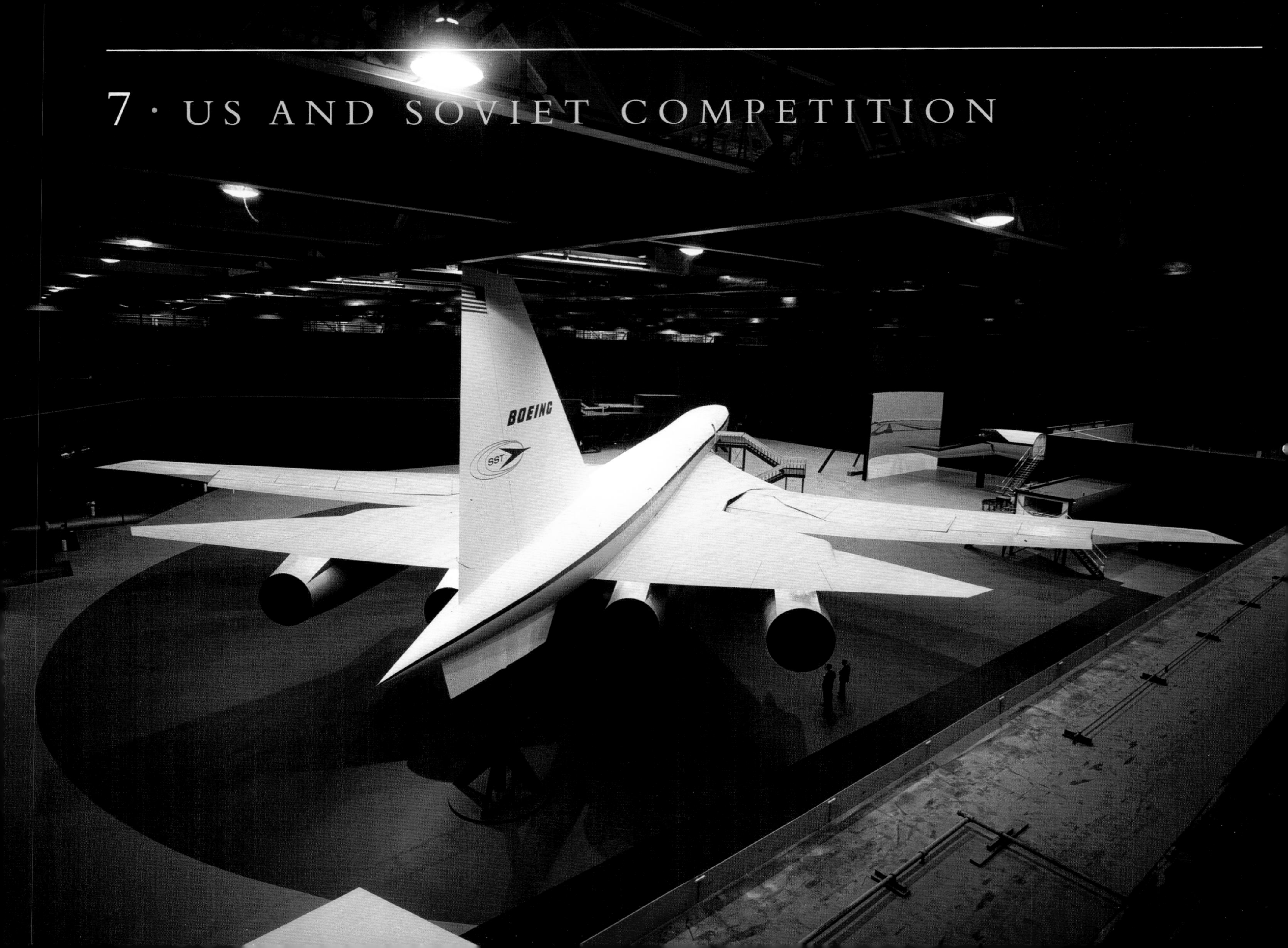

Left: A photograph of the full scale mock-up of the Boeing 2707. In June 1963 President Kennedy established the National Supersonic Transport programme, with the US Government funding 75 per cent of the development costs for a much larger aircraft than Concorde. Three aircraft firms bid for the project and Boeing won with its 306 feet long Boeing 2707 intended to carry 277 passengers flying at Mach 2.7–3.0 with a transatlantic range of 4,000 miles. This amazing design had variable-geometry wings and engines installed under the tail. (Boeing)

Right: The Boeing 2707 was to have seven-abreast seating with twin aisles – two seats each side with three in the centre. The mock-up was fitted with 277 seats (30 first-class and 247 tourist). The impression on entering the cabin was that at even its narrowest part the fuselage was noticeably wider than contemporary jet transports. (Boeing)

WITH the agreement by Britain and France to go ahead with an SST in 1962, the United States and the Soviet Union were eager to embark on similar programmes. Both nations had well-developed aviation industries with substantial supersonic experience.

The American attempt

In June 1963 President Kennedy established the National Supersonic Transport Programme with the US Government offering to fund 75 per cent of the cost of developing a competitor to Concorde. It was decided that the American SST should not seek to replicate Concorde but should instead outstrip it in size, range and performance. It was intended to carry 250 passengers at Mach 2.7–3.0 and have a transatlantic range of 4,000 miles, performance criteria which greatly increased complexity and cost. By choosing a maximum speed above Mach 2.2 the American manufacturers had set themselves the challenge of building an aircraft made from stainless steel or titanium.

Three US manufacturers were directed to bid for the project: Boeing, Lockheed and North American. Boeing was the winner with its 2707-200 design. It envisaged an aircraft 306 ft long, powered by either Pratt and Whitney JTF17A or General Electric GE4/J5 engines with a maximum speed of Mach 2.7.

This was a hugely ambitious project. Its variable geometry wings would be swept forward to 20 degrees to provide low speed for landing and swept back to 72 degrees for high speed flight. In their fully aft position the wings merged with the tailplane to give an overall delta configuration. Owing to concerns about jet blast, the four engines were actually mounted on the large tailplane.

The fuselage was planned to be of varying width. At its widest it was to be capable of seven abreast seating with two seats each side and three in the centre and two aisles. The 2707 mock-up was fitted with 277 seats: 30 first-class and 247 economy class.

But Boeing realised it was too complex, mainly because of the weighty jacks for the wing sweep mechanism. This fanciful design was superseded by the Boeing 2707-300, a more conventional delta design reminiscent of Lockheed's rejected proposal.

Although the Boeing SST had collected 115 options at a time when Concorde had only 74, it encountered substantial and growing opposition from politicians and environmental pressure groups. US politicians saw no reason why the aircraft

should be subsidised by the state for private profit and in May 1971 it was cancelled.

The Tupolev Tu-144 or 'Concordski'

In contrast to the Americans who failed to get a supersonic airliner airborne, the Soviet Union can be given credit that their SST took to the skies and briefly entered service, though it proved to have substantial technical flaws and was soon withdrawn from use.

In fact, the Tupolev Tu-144 made its maiden flight on the last day of 1968, beating Concorde into the air by more than three months with the maiden flight of the world's first supersonic airliner. On 5 June 1969 it became the first airliner to break the sound barrier and reached Mach 2 on 15 July 1969, again ahead of Concorde.

The Tu-144 bore a superficial resemblance to Concorde with its delta wing and droop nose but lacked its sophistication and underwent huge alterations in its configuration before entering service. The first prototype featured four engines grouped together under the fuselage centre section and had an ogival wing but without Concorde's camber. At what must have been great cost these features were modified on the Tu-144S where the engines were separated into two pairs and situated like Concorde's under each wing. The main undercarriage, however, remained in the same position as on the initial aircraft and so had to retract into the engine fairings. The fuselage was lengthened, the wing was replaced with a double-delta wing with conical camber and, to improve control, small retractable canard (or forward) control surfaces were added just behind the nose on either side of the aircraft, to increase lift and control at low speeds. These canard wings were only extended during low-speed flight and retracted into the side of the nose behind the flight deck at higher and supersonic speed.

Whereas the initial Tu-144 could reach Mach 2.15, this speed could only be maintained using reheat continuously, in contrast to Concorde which only used reheat at take-off and when accelerating to supersonic speed. This severely reduced the Tu-144's range owing to the amount of fuel consumed. The final version of the Tu-144, the Tu-144D, was a much improved version of the Tu-144S, employing better-developed engines which allowed it to replicate Concorde's use of reheat and doubled the aircraft's range.

A total of 16 Tupolev Tu-144s were completed between 1965 and 1984 in four different versions: the prototype, a pre-production Tu-144S and nine production Tu-144S models, followed by five Tu-144Ds. Unfortunately, while demonstrating at the Paris Air Show on 3 June 1973 a Tu-144S taking part in the flying display crashed, killing all on board and a number on the ground.

Three Tu-144s entered limited service with the Soviet state airline, Aeroflot, on regular flights between Moscow and Alma-Ata, Kazakhstan between 1975 and 1978, with a final flight on 1 June 1978 after just 102 passenger flights. In 1993 the last Tu-144D built was taken out of storage and after extensive modification given a limited lease of life as test bed on a joint supersonic transport research programme shared between Tupolev, NASA and other US firms, making a total of 27 flights between November 1996 and February 1998.

Some of the Tu-144s remain stored in Russia but one is preserved adjacent to an Air France Concorde at the Auto & Technik Museum in Sinsheim, Germany.

Concorde versus the Russian and American supersonic airliners

Unlike the Tupolev Tu-144 Concorde featured 'fly-by-wire' auto-stabilisation which put it ahead of any other commercial aircraft. As it had superb handling characteristics there was no need for the Tu-144's

The Tu-144S CCCP 77102 at the Paris Air Show on 3 June 1973 shortly before its fatal crash. The Tu-144S was substantially modified in contrast with the prototype; alterations included repositioning the engines and the introduction of foreplanes which were used for slow-speed flying and retracted against the side of the forward fuselage behind the cockpit when not in use. (BAE SYSTEMS)

The final appearance of the Tu-144 at the Paris Air Show was by CCCP 77144 in 1975. Note the foreplanes extended. (BAE SYSTEMS)

canard wings for lateral stability owing to its carefully conceived shaping of the wing. Though Concorde underwent considerable alterations between the first prototypes and the service aircraft, this was far less than the extensive metamorphosis that the Soviet aircraft underwent.

The much larger and faster Boeing SST never progressed beyond the drawing board and so no real comparison can be made. Doubtless its much higher speed and greater size would have caused far greater problems than those that had to be solved by Concorde's engineers.

While Britain and France were occupied in building Concorde, across the pond in Seattle the world's first 'Jumbo Jet', the subsonic

Boeing 747, was being prepared for its first flight, which took place on 9 February 1969. The difference in approach is elegantly explained in a fuel/passenger ratio; in contrast to Concorde, which could only manage 17 mpg per passenger, a 747 could carry four times the number of passengers on the same amount of fuel. The Boeing 747 is still in production at the time of writing (2008) while both the Anglo-French and Soviet SSTs have become museum pieces. It was only in 2007 that the Boeing 747 had real competition with the entry into service of the even larger Airbus A380, which can achieve 100 mpg per passenger.

THE first Concorde commercial services began with simultaneous departures from London and Paris at 11:40 hrs on 21 January 1976. British Airways' G-BOAA flew non-stop to Bahrain while Air France's F-BVFA took a route from Paris to Rio de Janeiro via Dakar.

Neither of these destinations had been envisaged for Concorde but the aircraft had been unable to fly into the United States thanks to vehement protests from the environmental lobby. Yet both airlines and manufacturers maintained the expectation that at some point in 1977 Concorde would not only be operating into the USA but also to Montreal, Tokyo and Johannesburg.

The inaugural French route to Rio, which took seven hours, was followed by a further one to South America with services to Caracas and Venezuela via the Azores. The British Airways route to Bahrain required the aircraft to cruise subsonically to Venice and then accelerate to Mach 2 halfway down the Adriatic, crossing the coast near Beirut and overflying Syria at supersonic speed, arriving in Bahrain 3 hrs 37 mins after leaving Heathrow. Bahrain was chosen as BA's initial destination because it was seen as the first leg of a possible route to Melbourne via Singapore. The cost of a single ticket was £352, £61 more than the subsonic first-class fare.

Concorde had received royal approval when, as part of her 1977 Silver Jubilee celebrations, the Queen flew on the aircraft from Barbados to London after completing an official state visit to Canada and the Caribbean. The 4,176-mile flight took just 3 hrs 45 mins.

In December 1977 the airline extended the Bahrain route to Singapore but was only able to operate it three times before the Malaysian Government refused overflying permission. There were several grounds, one of which was that fish in the Malacca Straits might have their breeding habits upset by the supersonic boom. Following further negotiations with the Malaysian Government, on 24 January 1979 British Airways began a joint operation to Singapore via Bahrain in co-operation with Singapore Airlines. The service involved Concorde G-BOAD being painted in Singapore Airlines' livery on its left-hand side with that of BA on the right. Although the flight crew were all from BA, the cabin crew alternated between the two airlines.

Initial expectations of high demand were not matched by actual load factors as, by 1979, Boeing 747s were flying London–Singapore non-stop in 13 hours. Concorde took nine hours with a refuelling stop in Bahrain and the service was discontinued at the beginning of November 1980.

Into the United States

The US Congress had initially banned Concorde landings in the United States, ostensibly bowing to public protests over sonic booms, delaying the launch of the lucrative transatlantic routes.

But then the position was eased when US Transportation Secretary William T. Coleman decided to allow trial services into Washington from 4 February 1976 for a period of 16 months. Regular services from both London and Paris to Washington Dulles Airport began on 24 May 1976. The inaugural arrival of the French and British Concordes was carefully planned for maximum effect and they landed virtually simultaneously on parallel runways. They then halted either side of the airport's huge pagoda-like control tower where 8,000 people had gathered to see them.

Actual experience proved to the American public that Concorde was less noisy than it had been generally expected to be. It was noisier than a 707 on take-off but quieter on landing and acceptance grew quickly. But gaining admittance to the more profitable and premier destination of New York's JFK airport took another 18 months to achieve because of the concerted opposition of pressure groups.

BA's intention was to extend its London–Bahrain service on to Singapore. After just three round trips in late 1977 the service was discontinued owing to objections by the Malaysian Government, but it was restarted in January 1979 when BA began a joint operation with Singapore Airlines using G-BOAD (seen taking off from Heathrow), which carried Singapore Airlines livery on its left side. (Carl Ford)

The battle for New York

The US ban on Concorde operations into JFK was lifted in February 1977. But the New York Port Authority had prohibited Concorde while noise levels were measured at Paris, London and Washington. This matter became a *cause célèbre*, eventually reaching the Supreme Court which finally lifted the Port Authority's local ban on 17 October 1977.

The manufacturers speedily responded and Concorde 201 F-WTSB began proving flights into New York on 19 October 1977. It was welcomed by huge crowds as well as by groups of protesters. Actual noise measurements at JFK proved Concorde to be within the legal limits on approach. On departure a special technique was employed requiring a 25-degree banking turn over the coast and away from populated areas. Opposition collapsed and services began on 22 November 1977 – this great metropolis soon became the favoured destination for Concorde passengers. Less than a year later, on 10 August 1978, the five BA Concordes then in operation carried their 100,000th passenger.

Services with Braniff

In co-operation with US airline Braniff International, British Airways and Air France offered an extension to their Washington services with a subsonic link to Dallas-Fort Worth Airport. But first Concorde had to obtain its US Certificate of Airworthiness, which was duly granted on 9 January 1979. Actual flights started three days later. Although the Concordes continued to display BA and Air France liveries, Braniff crews actually flew the aircraft. They had even gained supersonic experience although this was never used on flights between Washington and Dallas as the service was entirely overland.

For these services the aircraft also carried US registrations. This meant that, for example, BA's G-BOAA was re-registered as G-N94AA with the 'G' taped over when operating the Braniff services. Likewise, Air France's F-BVFC became N94FC. Most of the other Air France and British Airways Concordes were similarly identified. However, load factors on this service were never very high and at the beginning of June 1980 both airlines discontinued the Washington–Dallas Fort Worth route. Air France discontinued its Paris–Washington flights in March 1981.

Meanwhile, Air France announced the cessation of its inaugural route to Rio, first served in 1976, as well as its Caracas route, ending services in April 1982. Load factors on the Rio route had stabilised at 65 per cent, while it was just 40 per cent on the Caracas route. In neither case was it enough to make the services profitable. In November Air France further cut back its Concorde offerings and axed its twice-weekly services to Mexico City, which had been operated as extensions of its Paris–New York route. Consequently, from 1982 Air France's only scheduled service was its regular operation between Paris and New York. With the reduction in its Concorde route network Air France had insufficient work for seven aircraft. In May 1982 Concorde F-BVFD was withdrawn from service and later broken up. This aircraft was chosen as it had suffered a heavy landing at Dakar in 1977. The repair had increased its weight, resulting in a reduction in payload.

Between 1984 and 1991, British Airways flew a thrice-weekly Concorde service between London and Miami, stopping at Washington. The Dulles to Miami leg was flown subsonically, followed by a very rapid climb to 60,000 ft and acceleration to Mach 2, which was possible due to the aircraft's very light weight. It had less than one-third of its passenger complement on board and just enough fuel for the short Dulles–Miami sector. After about 6 to 8 mins at Mach 2 there was deceleration followed by descent into Miami.

Over 8,000 people came to Washington Dulles Airport to see the joint arrival of the BA and Air France Concordes on 24 May 1976 at the start of their 16 month trial period. BA recorded 93.3 per cent load factors on initial flights to this destination. (BAE SYSTEMS)

A bird's-eye view of the Concordes' triumphant arrival at Washington. (BAE SYSTEMS)

On several occasions bad weather at Dulles and a relatively light passenger payload out of Miami enabled non-stop Miami–London sectors to be flown. The fastest such flight took just 3 hrs 47 mins to fly over 4,000 nm from Miami to London with 70 passengers. The flight plan was filed to Shannon, Ireland, with *en route* re-clearance on to London secured after it had been established that the minimum required fuel for London was available.

In spite of these limited services and the small number of aircraft in operation, the aircraft in both airlines' Concorde fleets completed five years of service in January 1981, having logged a total of 15,800 flights and carried 700,000 passengers.

Disentangling government involvement

In 1981, after more than five years' service and the end of production, the division of responsibilities between the Governments, manufacturers and airlines required clarification even though the aircraft had proved itself technically.

The British and French Governments commissioned joint studies on the future of Concorde and ministers from both countries met in London to study three options for the future of Concorde proposed by officials. The options were:

■ Cancellation from 1 April 1982
■ A phased run-down
■ Indefinite continuation

Tortuous negotiations resulted in a decision that operations should continue. In March 1984 BA and Air France took over full financial responsibility for the aircraft and spares. As a result, BA paid £16.5m to the Government and acquired spares worth £120m, all seven Concordes plus the partly-cannibalised G-BBDG, which had been grounded at Filton as an additional spares source. Owing to the small size of the fleet, spares were only ordered in small quantities and even unserviceable parts were kept in case they had to be re-manufactured. The purchase of G-BBDG paid dividends for BA, allowing it to speedily replace the damaged rudder of G-BOAF when part of it became detached during the Christchurch, New Zealand to Sydney leg of a round-the-world flight in April 1989. When the nose visor of G-BOAF developed a problem it was exchanged for that of 'DG.

to axe Concorde. That proved to be far from the case. In 1983 he appointed Colin Marshall (later Lord Marshall) as BA's chief executive. Marshall was determined to emphasise Concorde's role as the airline's flagship. The interiors were revamped and fares increased to emphasise the exclusive nature of the supersonic airliner.

Concorde fares had originally been pitched at near first-class levels on conventional jetliners. Now they were raised to a level more than 30 per cent above first-class rates. The marketing message was refined to promote the superiority and convenience of Concorde's speed in addition to the excellence of the food and wine served on board.

As Concorde crossed the Atlantic in approximately 3.5 hrs, half the time taken by conventional airliners, BA promoted a one-day London–New York round trip to top British business travellers. Passengers could leave London Heathrow on the 10:30 hr Concorde, arrive at New York Kennedy at 9:30 hrs for business, then return to London on the 13:45 hr departure.

Because of its speed Concorde was able to outrun the Earth's rotation. On westbound flights it was possible to arrive at a local time ahead of the flight's departure time. On certain early-evening transatlantic flights departing from Heathrow or Paris, it was possible to take off just after sunset and catch up with the sun to land in daylight. This was much publicised by British Airways, which promoted the slogan 'Arrive before you leave.'

Air France also capitalised on the speed dividend when it organised a publicity stunt in which a 747 and a Concorde left Paris simultaneously for Boston. The Concorde flew to the US and returned to Paris before the 747 had even landed in Boston.

This new marketing strategy paid dividends. The 100-seat Concordes flew at well above the break-even point, achieving load

Left: After the New York Port Authority's resistance to Concorde was quashed by the US Supreme Court it was speedily arranged for F-WTSB to visit. It is seen here being towed into a hangar on 19 October 1977. In the forefront there are manufacturers and airline representatives about to be quizzed at a rather hostile press conference. From the left these are: McKinlay (BAC Deputy Director Flight Test), Dudal (AF Captain), Walpole (BA Captain), Franchi (Aérospatiale Director of Flight Test), Perrier (Aérospatiale Chief Engineer). (BAE SYSTEMS)

Marketing Concorde

In its early years of service with BA, Concorde was operated at a loss and attracted criticism from some sections of the British press which regarded the project as a white elephant. On one point everybody agreed: the iconic status and charisma of the aircraft. BA exploited Concorde's unique appeal to woo business customers, guaranteeing a certain number of Concorde upgrades in return for corporate accounts with the airline. This acted as a key factor in winning business from transatlantic competitors.

John King (later Lord King), who was appointed by Mrs Thatcher's Conservative Government to privatise the state-owned airline, might have been regarded as the hard-nosed businessman who would seek

Above: G-BOAA landing at Las Vegas during Braniff proving trials on 10-14 December 1978. The aircraft was flown throughout by Braniff crews, visiting 16 US cities, and was viewed by 25,000 people. (BAE SYSTEMS)

The joint arrival at New York JFK of Air France and British Airways Concordes on 22 November 1977 starting supersonic services between Paris, London and the 'Big Apple', which proved the longest-lasting Concorde-scheduled service. (BAE SYSTEMS)

factors of 60 per cent on Atlantic routes. The clientele was typically the corporate decision-makers which every airline courted.

When BA followed Air France in dropping its Washington service in November 1994, Concorde operations eventually settled down with both airlines only operating into New York. BA, however, bolstered this with a run to Barbados during the winter months, although the restricted range required careful fuel management by the crew on the four-hour sector to Barbados. However, Concorde was not only known for its scheduled operations because its cachet made charter operations extremely popular.

For BA, Concorde's main market remained the twice-daily New York return service which provided 90 per cent of the profit, while approximately 5 per cent of the revenue came from the Barbados operations and another 5 per cent from charters. Although 80 per cent of passengers on the New York route originated either from the USA or Britain, the remaining 20 per cent had flown to London from other countries to connect with the Concorde service.

Charters

Concorde's cachet also brought a new market sector within its remit and charter flights were to prove extremely popular. BA had initially been reluctant to employ Concorde on such operations as some within the airline felt it would weaken the exclusiveness of the brand. But the arrival of John King and Colin Marshall changed that attitude. In 1985 BA's Concordes flew 200 charters, with Air France aircraft operating approximately 70.

Several travel firms promoted special tours. For example, Goodwood Travel ran successful trips to Nice for the Monaco Grand Prix. The 20th anniversary of Concorde's maiden flight was celebrated by charters to Toulouse operated by both BA and Air France Concordes flying from Heathrow. Between 1983 and 2000 Goodwood Travel flew some 100,000 passengers to more than 50 destinations on Concordes. Some charters were comparatively short trips like supersonic tours of the Bay of Biscay, while others might involve a trip to Moscow to watch the Bolshoi Ballet.

Travellers were also happy to sign up to round-the-world flights. The first, in November 1986, involved a 28,249 mile trip from London westbound to New York, San Francisco, Honolulu, Guam, Hong Kong, Bali and Cairo. The total flying time was a mere 29 hrs 59 mins. The following month an Air France Concorde made a much more leisurely circumnavigation of the globe with an 18-day tour from Paris via New York, Oakland, Honolulu, Papeete, Sydney, Jakarta, Bangkok, Colombo, Bahrain and back to Paris.

On 12-13 October 1992, to commemorate the 500th anniversary of Columbus's landing in the New World, Concorde Spirit Tours chartered Air France's F-BTSD and circumnavigated the globe in 32 hrs 49 mins 3 secs, flying from Lisbon. Six refuelling stops were made, at Santo Domingo, Acapulco, Honolulu, Guam, Bangkok and Bahrain.

Rudder problems

The fifth round-the-world flight by G-BOAF in September 1989 was made all the more memorable by the loss of part of the upper rudder section on the leg from Auckland to Sydney. The tour was only delayed by 19 hrs thanks to some fast work by BA engineers. A replacement upper rudder section was taken from G-BBDG and flown out to

Sydney where it was quickly painted and fitted. The cause of the loss was water ingress causing delamination. Further failures followed in 1991 and 1992. In May 1991 BA announced it was to replace the upper and lower rudders on all its fleet. However, this did not prove the final answer to the problem. In 1998 G-BOAC lost part of an aileron and, later the same year, part of the replacement rudder. In 2002 BA suffered another rudder loss and in March 2003 Air France suffered its first rudder failure.

British Airways Concorde one-way fares
London–Bahrain January 1976: £356
London–Washington March 1976: £352
London–New York November 1977: £431
London–New York July 2003: £4,620 (return £6,999)

Concorde fares were typically 15 to 20 per cent higher than normal first class BA fares (British Airways)

Movie Star

The successful series of films began with the 1970 hit *Airport*, the first sequel to which was *Airport 1975*, a genuine blockbuster disaster movie with an all-star cast and an extensive promotional campaign. Its success led naturally to *Airport '77* and *Concorde...Airport '79*, by which time the

The first Concorde rudder loss was on the Christchurch to New Zealand leg of a round-the-world charter flight, but it caused no problem to the handling of the aircraft. Following further such incidents BA replaced all its Concorde rudders. (British Airways)

Right: For the joint services with Braniff both Air France and BA Concordes carried new registrations. G-BOAD in its partial Singapore Airlines livery was registered as G-N94AD and when operating the Braniff services the 'G-' was taped over, giving it an American registration. (Bristol Aero Collection)

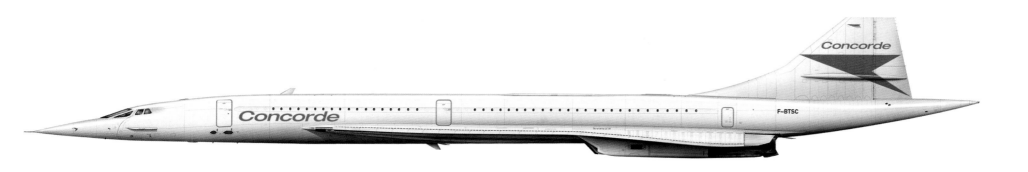

The special livery briefly worn by F-BTSC for its starring role in the film 'Airport 80 – Concorde'. (Rolando Ugolini)

concept had run its course and the reviews were unenthusiastic. Changing tack, Universal decided to re-market it as a comedy. Renamed *Concorde Airport 80* for UK release, it reached British cinemas a year later.

The plot involves an arms dealer, played by Robert Wagner, who attempts to destroy an American-owned Concorde on its maiden flight after one of the passengers learns of his weapons sales to communist countries during the Cold War. But the Concorde captain manoeuvres the aircraft so deftly that it escapes destruction from remotely-controlled missiles and rogue fighter aircraft. The arms dealer attempts

to depressurize the aircraft at altitude, forcing it to crash in the Alps.

The fifth Concorde built, F-BTSC, was leased from Aérospatiale to feature in the film and appeared in a special one-off livery before being sold to Air France in October 1980.

Ad star: Pepsi Max Supersonic

In an unusual and innovative relaunch of its brand, soft drinks giant Pepsi herded hundreds of journalists on to trains and transported them to a deserted aircraft hangar at Gatwick on 2 April 1996 to act as observers in the war between two global brands seeking international

Superb shot of F-BTSD landing at Dublin on 3 April 1996 in Pepsi livery during its tour of capitals to promote Pepsi's rebranding. The cost of repainting the Concorde was in the order of £100,000. (Carl Ford)

domination. Journalists from nearly 30 countries were brought together to watch Pepsi spend £300m on changing the colour of its cans from red and white to blue. Richard Brandt of Landor Associates, designers of the BA livery, had designed the new can and said blue had been chosen because it was most people's favourite colour.

With supermarket own-brands threatening to squeeze the cola market, the relaunch at a secluded part of Gatwick was planned with military precision. Foremost in the hype were two supermodels, Claudia Schiffer and Cindy Crawford, together with tennis star Andre Agassi. Pepsi's relaunch took the battle to the skies with the painting of Concorde F-BTSD in blue at an estimated cost of £100,000.

After a covert repaint in the Pepsi scheme, F-BTSD had left Orly on 31 March and then remained under wraps in a Gatwick hangar until the unveiling on 2 April. In its new blue livery, F-BTSD set off on a publicity tour visiting Dublin, Stockholm, Beirut, Dubai, Jeddah, Cairo, Milan and Madrid before returning to Paris on 9 April where it was finally returned to Air France livery.

A typical Concorde flight

The three flight deck crew gather 90 minutes before departure for a briefing on the weather and the flight plan. The two pilots board the cramped flight deck of the aircraft, joining the Flight Engineer who has performed the external checks. Following further briefings on procedures and information on the aircraft's weight distribution, take-off speeds are computed. Permission is requested from the Air Traffic Control (ATC) to start the engines. With permission granted, the pre-start check list commences. Engine number three and then number two are started and the Concorde is pushed back to the taxiway as the remaining two Olympuses are started. On the taxiway the tug disconnects from the nosewheel of the aircraft and Concorde taxies out towards the runway.

During this procedure the pre-take-off checks take place, ATC gives departure clearance and routeing and when Concorde reaches the holding point of the runway the aircraft halts, awaiting permission to take off. Once permission is granted the aircraft turns on to the runway, lines up, the pilot in command calls 'Standby 3, 2, 1, now' and the throttles are opened and Concorde accelerates. At 60 knots reheat is engaged automatically and when the V1 speed of 160 knots (the exact speed varies according to the aircraft's weight) is reached the pilot is

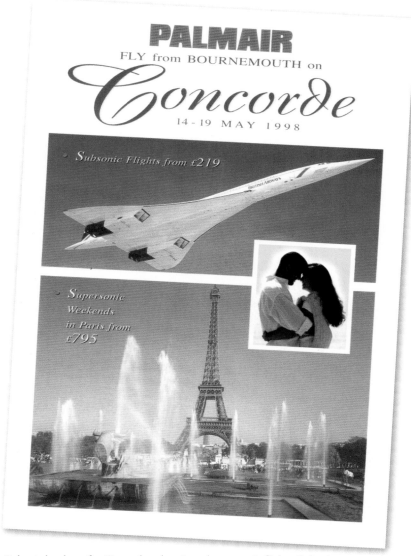

Palmair brochure for Concorde subsonic and supersonic flights. Palmair marketed flights from Bournemouth to New York and other destinations and shrewdly even sold the subsonic positioning flights of Concorde from Heathrow to Bournemouth, guaranteeing customers a flight of at least 25 minutes and a glass of champagne. (Mike Phipp)

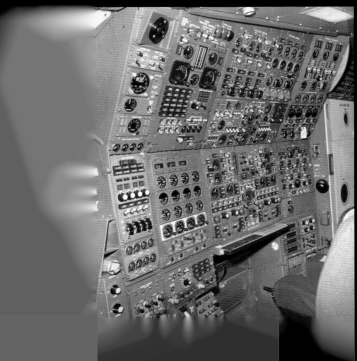

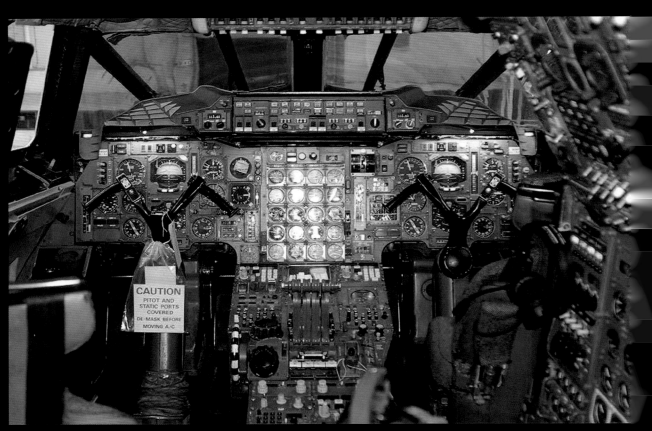

Left: The cramped Concorde flight deck, with the two pilots at the front, the Flight Engineer on the right and an additional crewman on the left occupying the supernumerary seat. (BAE SYSTEMS)

A close-up of the Flight Engineer's panel. (BAE SYSTEMS)

The pilots' instrument panel and the distinctive ram's-horn control columns. (Author's collection)

committed to take-off as there will be insufficient runway remaining in which to stop. Closely following V1 there is Vr, rotation speed, and as the pilot pulls back the ram's horn control column to raise the elevons, the aircraft climbs away at a 15° angle and the undercarriage is retracted. At 2,000 ft and at a speed of 250 knots reheat is cancelled for noise abatement procedures and the visor is fully raised.

Overland the Concorde accelerates and climbs under ATC control to Mach 0.95. On starting transonic acceleration, well clear of land, the throttles are opened; reheat is selected on the engines in pairs, firstly the inner two and then the outer two, to preserve a smooth ride for the passengers. As this happens fuel is transferred from the forward tank to wing and rear tanks to adjust the centre of gravity owing to the movement of the centre of lift during supersonic flight. Concorde then typically climbs to 60,000 ft above other air traffic. At transonic speed the air intakes come into operation creating a shock wave across the face of the intake slowing the flow of air into the engines to subsonic speeds. At Mach 1.7 the reheat is selected off and the engines alone will power the aircraft to Mach 2 (1,350 mph). Once settled into the cruise the crew continue to monitor the aircraft's performance and follow weather reports in case a diversion to another airport may be necessary. Meanwhile in the cabin the stewards and stewardesses busy themselves looking after the passengers.

Concorde was undoubtedly an extremely high performance machine. Flying at 23 miles per minute required tactical handling by the pilot in order, for example, to avoid placing a sonic boom overland. Pilots loved flying Concorde, not only for its prestige but because it was great to fly and could be flown comfortably just like another airliner.

As the aircraft consumed fuel at a high rate, fuel management was a critical factor in all aspects of the flight, whether supersonic or subsonic. But at subsonic speeds, owing to the much higher fuel consumption, range was halved. The autopilot and autothrottle were both simple to use, the former particularly useful when flying conditions were poor. Concorde was certified for full Category 3 autoland. This enabled the aircraft to be flown down to a height of only 15 ft above the runway threshold and if visibility was 200 metres ahead the crew would then manually land the aircraft. If not they would need to overshoot and fly to a diversionary airport.

When Concorde is ready to descend, the throttles are slowly retarded well ahead of land, fuel is transferred back to adjust the centre of gravity and IT decelerates to subsonic speeds, descending below 40,000 ft. Concorde is then directed through other traffic and lines up on final approach to the landing runway at 190 knots at 2,500 ft. As this happens the undercarriage is selected down and the visor lowered to 12½°. The visor allows the pilots to have a clear view of the runway as owing to Concorde's delta configuration it flies the approach at an angle of 11°, in contrast to 2° to 3° of most airliners. Speed is reduced and the Flight Engineer calls out the altitude from the radio altimeter until at 40 ft the autothrottle is disconnected and at 15 ft the throttles closed.

Landing at about 160 knots from a high angle of attack, sitting 97 ft in front of the main wheels, is not difficult for the crew to attain as the airlines provided excellent training. When the nosewheel is on the ground, reverse thrust is engaged, the brakes are applied and the control column pushed forward to keep the aircraft firmly on the ground. Reverse is then reduced to idle reverse on the outer and inner Olympuses in succession as speed falls and the Concorde taxies off the runway towards the stand. The nose is raised to 5° and the crew go through all their checks until shutdown and disembarkation of the passengers.

The passenger experience

Travelling by Concorde was different in many ways from flying on subsonic commercial airliners. Concorde passengers were paying for speed not super comfort. British Airways and Air France configured the passenger cabin on their supersonic airliners in a single class with 100 seats, two either side of a central aisle. Headroom in the central aisle was barely 6 ft. The leather seats were not overly generous and with leg room at a 38 in pitch it was only about 4 in more than that of economy class accommodation on a Boeing 747. With limited room for overhead storage, carry-on luggage was severely restricted. Flying at twice a conventional airliner's cruising altitude, the view from the windows clearly showed the curvature of the Earth and turbulence was rare.

Special paint protected Concorde from the heating generated by flying through the air at twice the speed of sound and thermal expansion caused by skin friction. While the outside air temperature was below -50 degrees C, the tip of the nose would reach 127 degrees C and the airframe would stretch by 6 in. Fuselage insulation shielded the passenger compartment from these harsh

extremes, ensuring that the occupants remained comfortably cocooned.

In the 1990s, features like video entertainment or reclining seats, common in the first and business class cabins on subsonic long-haul flights, were absent from Concorde. But the 3.5 hrs flight time from London to New York helped to make up for these deficiencies.

And there was an exceptionally high level of passenger service. Meals were served on specially-designed compact crockery, although the silver cutlery was replaced by plastic items for safety reasons after the 11 September 2001 terrorist attacks in the US.

Reheat engaged on all four Olympuses to accelerate Concorde to take-off speed. (Phil Jones)

A superb view of G-BOAC, the first Concorde delivered to BA, taking off. (BAE SYSTEMS)

G-BOAF, the last Concorde delivered to BA, climbing away and retracting its undercarriage. Note the visor is still at its 5° down position.
(BAE SYSTEMS)

Concorde G-BOAC banking and climbing away still with the visor down. (Rob Ware)

Right: A diagram plotting altitude against time indicating the brief use of reheat at take-off and its greater use to accelerate to supersonic speed as it climbs. (Rolls-Royce Historical Trust)

Far right: A diagram illustrating the operation of the engine intake system which managed the speed of the airflow into the engine, slowing it to subsonic speed even when the aircraft was flying at twice the speed of sound. In the event of an engine failure the ramps functioned in a different manner to dump air from the intake. (Rolls-Royce Historical Trust)

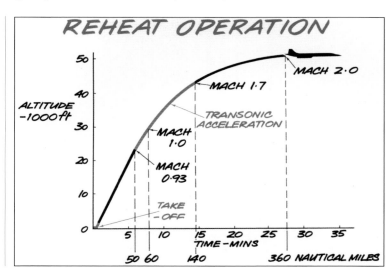

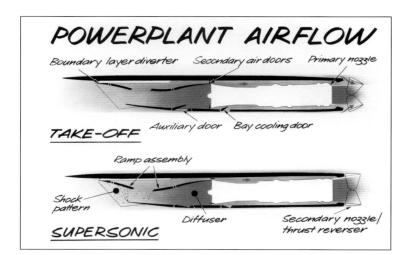

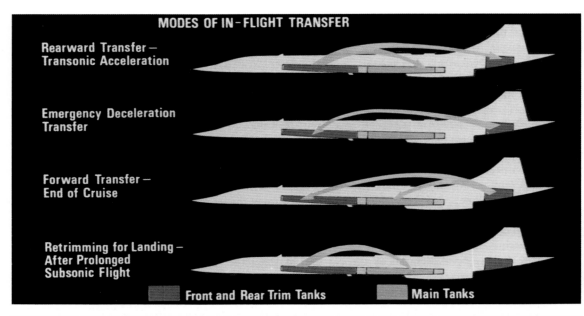

MODES OF IN-FLIGHT TRANSFER

Rearward Transfer –
Transonic Acceleration

Emergency Deceleration
Transfer

Forward Transfer –
End of Cruise

Retrimming for Landing –
After Prolonged
Subsonic Flight

Front and Rear Trim Tanks   Main Tanks

Owing to the change in the centre of gravity at supersonic speeds fuel was transferred during acceleration and deceleration. (BAE SYSTEMS)

BA Concorde cabin crew photographed in the passenger cabin. (Author's collection)

Left: Concorde about to land with the visor fully down to give the pilots a clear view of the ground even though the aircraft is at an angle of 12° to the ground. This photograph shows G-BOAF landing at the 1988 Farnborough Air Show. (Derek Ferguson)

This wonderful photograph of four Concordes was originally taken when BA airliners bore 'Landor' livery but was expertly retouched to the 'Chatham' livery. (British Airways)

A further most unusual livery was that worn by production prototype F-WTSB which was painted in this scheme at Toulouse to celebrate the 20th Anniversary of the maiden flight of Concorde in 1989. (BAE SYSTEMS)

British Airways Concordes often appeared together in formation with the RAF Red Arrows. Here is G-BOAG with the Hawks of the Red Arrows at Fairford on 15 July 1985. (Derek Ferguson)

A view of the seats installed in a BA Concorde and the small passenger windows. At the height at which Concorde flew the sky was a dark blue and the curvature of the Earth was visible. (Author's collection)

The Concorde passenger cabin, which carried 100 passengers in a four-abreast layout. Note the rather restricted size of the baggage lockers. (Author's collection)

BA Concorde ticket (Author's collection)

THE CONCORDE MENU

*Concorde menus
(Author's collection)*

Brunch

Appetiser

Caviar

Entrées

English breakfast featuring back bacon,
scrambled eggs, pork sausage, tomato and
mushrooms

Free-range chicken breast with black truffle,
foie gras, savoy cabbage and fondante potato

Lobster and saffron crushed potato cakes with
spinach and Bloody Mary relish

Fennel and orange salad with goats cheese
and pinenuts

Dessert

Mango and almond gratin

OR

Cheese

Stilton, Chevre and Pecorino with balsamic
vinegar

Selection of bread rolls

Coffee, decaffeinated coffee, a selection of tea
with chocolates

As an alternative to the full menu, we are
pleased to offer a selection of freshly made
sandwiches including chicken, egg and bacon,
rocket with goats cheese

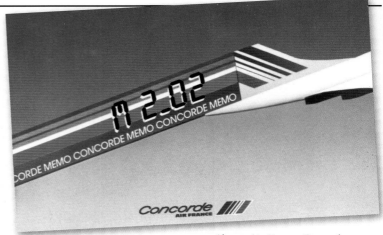

*Above: Air France Concorde
promotional notepad.*

CONCORDE
FLIGHT CERTIFICATE

PRESENTED TO

_____

WHO FLEW SUPERSONICALLY ON CONCORDE
BETWEEN

_____

ON

_____

Lord King of Wartnaby
Chairman

Sir Colin Marshall
Chief Executive

Captain

CONCORDE

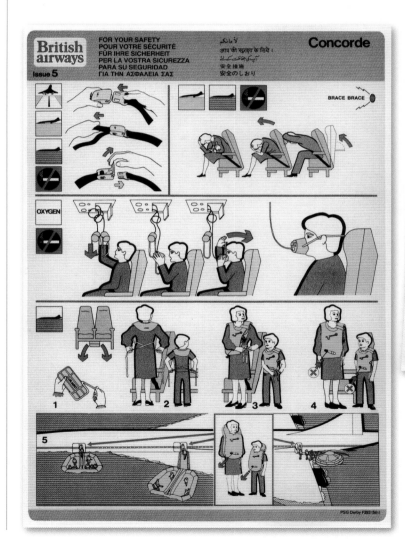

Left: BA and Air France issued Certificates to passengers to authenticate that they had flown on Concorde. The Certificate was signed by the Captain of the flight and bore the signatures of the airline's Chairman and Chief Executive. (Author's collection)

BA Concorde Emergency Escape chart (Author's collection)

F-BTSC taking off with a trail of flames and smoke caused by the ignition of the fuel pouring from a hole under its wing. On close examination of this photograph it is possible to see that the front inner main gear wheel tyre is missing and that unburnt fuel is flowing from the ruptured tank. This photograph was shot by a Japanese passenger on an Air France Boeing 747 with the French President Jacques Chirac on board, which was waiting to cross the runway once Concorde has passed.
(Associated Press)

The actual piece of metal on the runway which penetrated a tyre and caused pieces of it to damage the undercarriage and wing which led to the fuel leak and its ignition. (BEA)

THIS broad sequence of events describing the only fatal Concorde accident is set out in the French official accident report. It states that on Tuesday, 25 July 2000 Air France Concorde F-BTSC, Flight no. Air France 4590, was a charter flight taking a group of German holidaymakers from Paris-Charles De Gaulle Airport to New York, where they were to join a cruise.

Air France 4590 left the stand at 14:34 and taxied to the holding point of runway 26 right, arriving there at 14:40. Two minutes later the throttles were eased forward and reheat engaged. While accelerating during its take-off run F-BTSC ran over a strip of metal deposited on the runway by a Continental Airlines McDonnell Douglas DC-10. It cut into one of the left front mainwheel tyres, which immediately exploded. Large chunks of rubber were hurled upwards to the underside of the wing which caused a shockwave in a fuel tank, causing it to rupture from the inside. The venting fuel, estimated at up to 100 litres per second, ignited, immediately upsetting the performance of the two engines on the left side and causing them to surge. The Paris Control Tower warned the crew that the aircraft was on fire. But as the pilot had passed V1, the point where he would have sufficient runway length remaining in which to safely stop, and with the limited information he had available to him, he continued the take-off. Following the loss of power F-BTSC gradually drifted to the left of its track along the runway. When it rotated it was almost on the edge of the left side of the runway. It managed to take off lower than the normal rotation speed but was seen by onlookers trailing a huge plume of flames.

As the aircraft rotated, engine number 1 lost power through ingestion of fuel, and engine number 2's fire bell sounded owing to the alarm system's detection of a fire, actually an external fire. The Flight Engineer then shut engine number 2 down. Some damage had apparently been caused to the hydraulics because although undercarriage retraction was selected it failed to operate. The Concorde was now in a critical condition, barely able to make 200 knots at 200 ft. The crew radioed that they would try to make for Le Bourget Airport for a crash landing but the extended landing gear down was causing substantial drag and with power from only two of the engines the aircraft could not gain sufficient airspeed. The Concorde reared up and stalled, crashing on to 'La Patte d'Oie' Hotel in Gonesse, just west of the airfield. The time was 14:44, just less than three minutes after take-off, killing all 109 people on board and four on the ground. Only 80 seconds had elapsed from running over the strip of metal to the crash.

The aftermath

This crash was an appalling shock to Air France, which immediately cancelled all its Concorde flights. As a mark of respect British Airways followed suit by cancelling its service to New York that day although it resumed services on the next. BA flights then continued for three weeks until 15 August. G-BOAC was taxiing to take off for New York when the UK Civil Aviation Authority informed British Airways that as it appeared a single tyre burst had caused the crash, Concorde's Certificate of Airworthiness would be revoked. G-BOAC was ordered to return to the stand and Concorde services were suspended. The following day the French and British authorities officially withdrew Concorde's Certificate of Airworthiness. Both operators had aircraft stranded in New York which were then flown back to their respective bases without passengers to join the other members of their fleets.

There had been 12 incidents in Concorde's history in which tyre failure had led to damage to the wings or landing gear. In six cases there had been penetration of the wing tanks. The sequence of events that led to this, the only Concorde fatal accident was not unique except that on all the previous occasions there had been no fire.

Simulation after the accident of a Concorde tyre with a similar metal strip. (BEA)

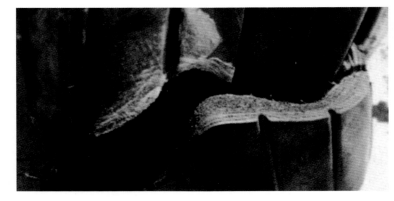

Cuts in a specimen tyre produced from running the tyre over the strip of specimen metal. (BEA)

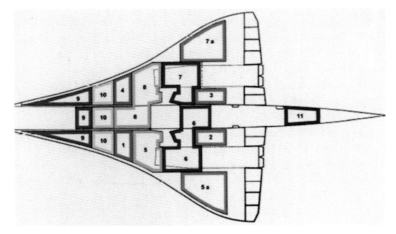

Left: There were various items of debris left by the Air France Concorde on the runway at Charles de Gaulle Airport, including a piece of F-BTSC's actual tyre which was recovered from the runway. (BEA)

Above: On the runway following the accident there was also a piece of the underside of the wing from fuel tank number 5. The verdict of the French accident report was that following the tyre running over the metal strip, a piece of the tyre impacted on the underside of the wings, which were absolutely full of fuel. The impact caused an over-pressure in the tank and a piece of the underside of the wing ruptured and fuel flowed out, which was ignited. (BEA)

Above left: A diagram of the Concorde's wing tanks, showing the position of tank 5 from where the substantial fuel leak developed. (BEA)

BEA (*Bureau Enquêtes-Accidents*), the French aircraft accident authority body, immediately began an investigation. It produced interim reports and then a final one in January 2002 which was published after Concorde had returned to service. This indicated that Concorde's vulnerability to tyre burst and the concomitant damage to the wing was the sole cause of the accident.

Continuing questions about the accident

Despite this conclusion there were a number of aspects that some commentators felt were given insufficient weight in the French report and raised questions as to whether an inherent weakness in the aircraft had been the sole cause.

- The aircraft was one tonne over its MTOW when it arrived at the threshold. This was because it had not burnt the estimated fuel when taxiing and the wind had become a moderate 8-knot tail wind. Some crews might have elected to taxi to the other end of the runway burning off more fuel to reduce weight and take off into the wind.
- Though Charles de Gaulle Airport staff were supposed to carry out three runway inspections a day, only one had taken place at the time of Concorde's take-off at 14:42.
- Why did the crew shut down Engine number 2 when the aircraft was only just off the ground? The Air France Flight Manual states that in the event of an engine fire the engine should not be shut down until 400 ft has been reached. With the loss of the power of Engine number 2 and the later actual failure of Engine number 1, F-BTSC had insufficient power to fly when the undercarriage failed to retract. But with engine 2 functioning the Concorde would have been able to maintain height and fly.
- During investigations by the BEA it was discovered that a spacer, a part of the left main undercarriage, was missing which may have exacerbated the aircraft's skew to the left during its take-off run.

Sooty marks on the runway showing where the ignition of the fire took place and the track of the Concorde as it started to veer left after the fire had started. (BEA)

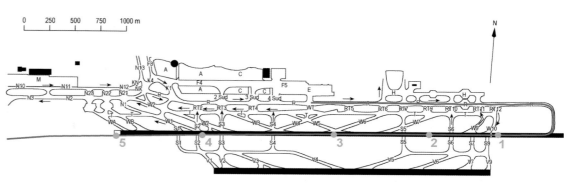

Above: The track of F-BTSC on the Southern runway at Charles de Gaulle Airport. The numbers refer to the following: 1 = 100 knots; 2 = V1 at 151 knots; 3 = Flames reported to the Concorde by Air Traffic Control at 184 knots; 4 = Concorde just airborne at 201 knots; 5 = Captain requests retraction of the undercarriage at 199 knots. (BEA)

Right: An aerial photograph indicating the brief final flight of F-BTSC from Charles de Gaulle Airport. (BEA)

Far right: An aerial view of the crash site at Gonesse, near Paris, where the Concorde came down tail first on the Hotelissimo Hotel, killing four of the staff. (BEA)

This may also explain Captain Marty's 11-knot early rotation of the aircraft in order to avoid running off the side of the runway.

However, it must be said that the crew were in an impossible position with insufficient information or time in which to recover the situation.

The solution

To regain certification the airworthiness authorities directed that the following modifications would need to be incorporated for it to fly again:

- ■ Kevlar linings, often employed in military aircraft and also used as body armour, were to be fitted to each vulnerable fuel tank to drastically reduce the rate of fuel leakage in the event of damage to the wing.

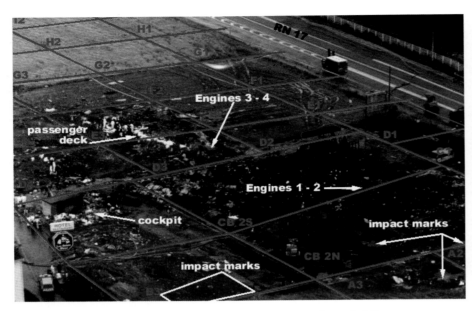

Left: Crash investigators comb through the wreckage. (BEA)

Below: One of the major modifications required in the re-certification of Concorde was the installation of Kevlar lining in any of the fuel tanks that might be vulnerable to damage from the tyres. In the event of a puncture of the tank the Kevlar lining would severely limit any outflow of fuel. Kevlar is similarly employed in military aircraft. This proved a challenging task for engineers as the tanks had not been designed for such access. (British Airways)

Above: Another aerial view indicating the positioning of the wreckage. (BEA)

Amidst the wreckage was the co-pilot's and the central instrument panel. (BEA)

At Warton a replica of the Concorde's undercarriage bay with the fractured wing fuel tank was fabricated and placed in the wind tunnel. The photograph on the left shows the punctured underwing fuel tank and undercarriage leg. The right-hand photograph shows the result of ignition of fuel. (BEA)

- fitting new Michelin tyres, designed to be more resilient to damage by foreign objects and to shed only lighter pieces of tread at a much lower level of energy.
- electrical wiring in the main landing gear bay to be given additional protection.
- The undercarriage water deflectors to be modified.
- functioning of the tyre pressure detectors and warning systems was mandatory, (i.e. the aircraft could not fly without these).
- electrical power to the brake cooling fans to be isolated for take off and landing.

The installation of these modifications began on five BA Concordes and three Air France Concordes. These modifications cost BA £17m per aircraft while the remodelling of the cabins with new weight-saving soft leather seats and subdued lighting designed by Terence Conran cost BA £2m per aircraft. This meant that although the aircraft's weight had increased with the post-crash modifications BA's Concordes were still able to carry a full payload. Air France chose not to emulate BA in revamping their cabins with lighter materials so had to limit their aircraft's capacity to 92 passengers.

Post-crash trials
The first Concorde to fly out of Paris was the unmodified F-BVFB which flew out amid emotional scenes on 18 January 2001 to the French military test airfield at Istres where it carried out special trials with coloured water and special nozzles mounted under the wings to identify where the original fuel leak had originated during the accident.

Rolls-Royce re-established a long-unused Olympus engine test rig at Shoeburyness in Essex to examine the engine's performance during the ingestion of fuel or gases. The results were positive and showed that when confronted with the quantities of fuel or gas present in the accident, the Olympus would surge but recover.

At BAE Systems Warton an example of the left undercarriage bay was fabricated to simulate and examine the fuel leak, ignition and propagation of the fire. However the accident investigators were unable to conclude whether the ignition was the result of electrical arcing from damaged undercarriage wiring or from the hot parts of the engine or the reheat.

A second Air France Concorde F-BTSD was flown to Istres on 11 April 2001 for trials with the new Michelin tyre in both dry and wet conditions. These tyres were lighter than the Goodyear or Dunlop examples being replaced and helped compensate for the increase in aircraft weight caused by the fitting of the Kevlar linings.

Post-modification flights
The first Concorde to incorporate the modifications stipulated by the airworthiness authorities was G-BOAF. Installation of these alterations was comparatively straightforward except for the fitting of Kevlar linings to those tanks deemed vulnerable to damage. The linings needed some individual tailoring to fit each aircraft and proved extremely challenging as BA had to select engineers small enough to enter fuel tanks which had never been designed for access.

Following a series of ground trials to check the functioning of all the equipment which had remained unused for virtually a year, G-BOAF flew out of Heathrow on 17 July 2001, piloted by BA Chief Concorde pilot Mike Bannister and Jock Reid, the CAA's Chief Test Pilot. Concorde routed out over the Atlantic accelerating to Mach 2 and landed at RAF Brize Norton. Three days later a flight of similar duration was made out of Brize Norton returning to Heathrow. The results of these flights proved that the Kevlar linings did not affect the fuel system's operation and Concorde could now re-enter service. Meanwhile the first Air France Concorde to be brought up to modification standard flew on 27 August and both airlines' engineers worked hard to carry out the modifications on the remaining Concordes and retrain the flight crews.

A British Airways Concorde in dock at Heathrow – major maintenance checks took place every 12,000 flight hours, taking approximately three months. All paint was removed as were the engines and internal fittings. Electrical cabling was replaced. (BAE SYSTEMS)

Left: A beautiful photograph of Concorde leaving Heathrow for New York. Concorde services to New York were resumed by both Air France and British Airways on 7 November 2001, following more than a year's grounding due to the accident in Paris and the withdrawal of the Airworthiness Certificate. (Rob Ware)

ON 5 September 2001 Concorde was re-certificated by the British and French airworthiness authorities and concrete plans could be set in train for the resumption of services. BA had missed out on £50m in lost profits and revenues while the Concorde fleet was grounded. BA's public relations team had worked to maintain close contact with a celebrity supersonic clientele which included Phil Collins, Sir Elton John, Sir Paul McCartney, Madonna, Sir Cliff Richard and Sting.

The airline released regular progress reports on its plans to return Concorde to service and hosted visits to the Heathrow hangars to allow press and interested parties to see the work at first-hand and to reassure them about the aircraft's safety. Senior figures in industry and banking, who were missing the time-saving flights, were among the first to take the opportunity to preview the improved Concordes.

Back to New York

BA and Air France resumed Concorde passenger flights on 7 November with celebrities, corporate customers and news media representatives travelling from London to New York. Alpha Echo was five minutes late when it left its stand at 10.35 hrs under grey cloudy conditions. But it was cheered on by BA engineers who had toiled for the past 15 months to make sure it could fly again. After take-off the aircraft reached 700mph over the Bristol Channel before achieving its top speed of 1,325 mph, 25 min after leaving Heathrow.

The guest list included Digby Jones, director general of the Confederation of British Industry, Sir David Frost, Sting and national newspaper editors like Piers Morgan of *The Mirror*. Rod Eddington, BA's chief

executive, said British business leaders had been invited on the flight to thank them for their support. 'Concorde is back and will be here for at least another decade,' he declared. Both airlines were initially providing one weekday service to New York and hoped to add a second by summer 2002.

Tony Benn, the former Minister of Technology who had fought for Concorde and had represented the British Government at the roll-out of the French prototype in 1968, was there to wave it off from Heathrow. He recalled that he had been responsible for agreeing to the French spelling of Concorde with an 'e'. On this occasion the BBC reported him as saying: 'E is for excellence and extravagance but it is such a graceful aircraft and it has also provided thousands of jobs for some of my old constituents in Bristol.'

Right: Air France's final Concorde F-BVFF at San Diego. This view shows the typical manner in which the elevons drooped when power was off. (Bristol Aero Collection)

New York joint arrival

After being grounded for more than a year, BA's G–BOAE and Air France's F–BVFB arrived at JFK just 50 min apart and parked nose-to-nose as a symbolic gesture of their joint return to commercial service. New York was overjoyed at the reunion. The city's mayor, Rudy Giuliani, went so far as to jump aboard BA's Alpha Echo to welcome it back. He told BA's invited passengers that the bonds which had always bound London and New York together had been reinforced after the events of 9/11 only two months earlier.

Within hours of the Alpha Echo's departure from Heathrow, Prime Minister Tony Blair was doing his bit by taking a second Concorde for a two-hour meeting with President Bush in Washington. He returned by breakfast time on 8 November, demonstrating that business people and politicians could benefit from using Concorde's speed.

Fare-paying flights resume

Flights carrying fare-paying flights resumed on 9 November and initial bookings appeared good. But fear of flying had taken on a whole new dimension following the 9/11 terrorist attacks. Security procedures were tightened throughout the airline industry and Concorde was no exception. Now the crew would be locked in the flight deck and there could be no more passenger visits to the flight deck. Even the cutlery was plastic.

After announcing the resumption of Concorde services, BA took bookings worth more than £20m up to Christmas 2001 from 7,200 passengers for its New York and Barbados services. As a special offer, BA tempted people with a £2,999 fare but soon reverted to the more usual £6,999 for a return flight from Heathrow to New York. With plenty of life remaining in the fleet the initial expectation within BA was that Concorde would fly for many more years.

But the climate had changed drastically in the aftermath of 9/11. Before the July 2000 crash, BA's top dozen corporate clients – the big investment banks and multinationals like GlaxoSmithKline and BP – had Concorde flights included in their packages.

When Concorde resumed flying in November 2001, the number of prospective passengers had dwindled considerably from Concorde's heyday when the aircraft typically flew three-quarters full. In those days BA earned an annual £20m in operating profits from its 35,000 Concorde passengers. With the return to service, paying almost £7,000 to fly supersonic had lost its appeal. BA could attract sufficient business

for only one transatlantic flight a day instead of the previous two. Even then the aircraft was often not very full and extra seats were often occupied by upgrading subsonic first-class and business-class customers.

Concorde had not lost its allure for some leisure travellers, however. When BA offered seats for a special 2002 New Year return flight to New York to celebrate the arrival of 2002 they reportedly sold out within three minutes. And at the beginning of December 2002 G-BOAF relaunched the Saturday-only service to Barbados which had been a regular part of the winter timetable since its introduction in 1987.

Concorde's life extension

BA had spent approximately £20m on the 'Re-life 1' maintenance programme for five of its seven Concordes between 1996 and 1998. This would have enabled them to fly until 2009 upon reaching 8,500 supersonic cycles. An additional cost of about £36m would have taken BA's entire fleet of seven Concordes to 10,000 supersonic cycles under 'Re-life 2' and would have extended its service life from 2008 to 2013. After that, a 'Re-life 3' programme was envisaged. As Air France had never implemented the initial 'Re-life 1' for its own Concorde fleet, it had previously announced that it planned to retire its Concorde fleet in 2007.

Air France Concorde incidents

When the British Government had wanted to withdraw from the programme it was the French Government which had refused to follow suit. But Air France's commitment to Concorde had never been as enthusiastic as BA's. Air France's highest-time Concorde had flown fewer hours than even BA's lowest-hour example. Then the airline reduced services to one regular round trip flight per day to JFK when two incidents in close succession made a serious impact on the French fleet.

On 19 February 2003 F-BTSD was operating the scheduled Paris–New York service when a fuel leak was noticed in engine number 3. When the crew shut down this engine, they failed to turn off the valve controlling fuel flow to it. After suddenly noticing an alarming drop in the remaining fuel, the captain diverted to Halifax, Nova Scotia for an emergency landing with very little fuel remaining, narrowly averting another potentially fatal accident.

G-BOAC is preserved at the Manchester Airport Museum and arrived on 31 October 2003. It is seen here taxiing in after its final flight. (Phil Jones)

On 3 November 2003 G-BOAG left Heathrow for the last time bound for Seattle, pausing at New York for a night stop and then supersonically over Canada. It is now preserved at the Museum of Flight in Seattle. (Paul Robinson)

Just eight days later, on 27 February, F-BVFA lost part of its rudder during its climb to altitude between Paris and New York. The cause was moisture contamination of the rudder's composite material, causing loss of integrity to the structure from freezing and thawing.

BA had encountered this problem on five occasions. The carrier had stepped-up hangar inspections of the external surfaces and had even replaced all the rudders in its Concorde fleet. This failed to prevent further problems. The shredding of the composite material stopped at the metal structure surrounding it and the rudder was mainly used on the ground. But these two incidents, together with the heavy maintenance costs and the likelihood of continuing operating losses resulting from low utilisation, gave support to those in Air France who wanted to see an end to Concorde operations.

After the joint announcement by the two airlines on 10 April 2003 that services would end, Virgin offered to buy the BA Concordes, but British Airways turned the offer down. Had Richard Branson's bid been accepted this is how Concorde would have appeared in Virgin livery. (Rolando Ugolini)

The end is announced

On 10 April 2003 British Airways and Air France simultaneously announced that they would retire Concorde later that year. They cited low passenger numbers following the 25 July 2000 crash, the slump in air travel after 9/11 and rising maintenance costs as the chief reasons for their decision.

Air France chairman Jean-Cyril Spinetta stated: 'Air France deeply regrets having to make the decision to stop its Concorde operations but it has become a necessity. The worsening economic situation in the last few months has led to a decline in business traffic which particularly weighs on Concorde's results. Maintenance costs have substantially increased since its return to service. Operating Concorde has become a severely and structurally loss-making operation. In these circumstances it would be unreasonable to continue operating it any longer.'

BA's Rod Eddington said: 'Concorde has served us well and we are extremely proud to have flown this marvellous and unique aircraft for the past 27 years. This is the end of a fantastic era in world aviation but bringing forward Concorde's retirement is a prudent business decision at a time when we are having to make difficult decisions right across

the airline. The demise of the Concorde will indeed be a sad day in aviation history, even the end of an era. If you have the means and the time, don't miss a last chance to fly aboard its majestic splendour.'

Virgin Concordes?

That same day Sir Richard Branson offered to buy British Airways' Concordes at their 'original price of £1' for service with his Virgin Atlantic Airways. Branson claimed this was the same token price that British Airways had paid the British Government. BA denied this and refused the offer.

Branson wrote in *The Economist* of 23 October 2003 that his final offer was 'over £5m' and that he had intended to operate the fleet 'for many years to come.' But any hope of Concorde remaining in service was further thwarted by Airbus' unwillingness to provide maintenance support for the aircraft.

Airbus statement

A press release from Noël Forgeard, president and chief executive officer of Airbus, stated: 'The Airbus predecessors, Aérospatiale and British Aircraft Corporation, created the Concorde some 40 years ago and we are proud of this remarkable achievement. But its maintenance regime is increasing fast with age. Thus, as an aircraft manufacturer, we completely understand and respect the decision of Air France and British Airways, especially in the present economic climate. It goes without saying that, until the completion of the very last flight, we will continue to support the operators so that the highest standards of maintenance and safety are entirely fulfilled.'

Background to the decision

Some commentators suggested that there was more to this decision than met the eye. Apparently Air France was anxious to end Concorde services but did not want to leave BA as the sole Concorde operator. It appears that Air France's intention gained support from Airbus, holders of design authority for Concorde, which then announced that the new extra cost of technical support over the subsequent five-year period would be £8m per year, or a total of £40m for both Air France and BA combined.

But if Air France retired its Concorde fleet the entire extra cost would have to be borne by BA alone. As BA services were then just one daily round-trip London–New York flight, the increased Airbus technical support bill would effectively remove the possibility that such reduced service would ever produce more than financial break-even. This left BA with no alternative but to cease Concorde operations.

The final Air France Concorde flights

Air France's final scheduled Concorde journey to New York was on Friday, 30 May 2003 when F-BTSD left Paris. On arrival at JFK, fire trucks stood by to meet it with a traditional water cannon salute. The following day, when the aircraft returned to Paris Charles de Gaulle,

it brought to a close 27 years of Air France Concorde operations. F-BTSD touched down at Charles de Gaulle Airport at 17:44 hrs, having flown over many thousands of enthusiasts gathered at the end of Runway 09.

While F-BTSD was in the air, a supersonic charter flight by F-BVFB took enthusiasts around the Bay of Biscay. This had been due to touch down minutes before the final passenger service from New York arrived. One of the 'FB's engines refused to start but after frantic activity by ground staff this was rectified and the aircraft departed an hour late. As a result `FB's passengers had the honour of travelling on the last ever supersonic commercial flight operated by Air France.

The flight landed at 18:30 hrs, the crew waving from the cockpit windows as the aircraft taxied past the crowds and headed towards Air France's corporate headquarters at the airport en route to Terminal 2.

BA's final Concorde extravaganza

While Air France speedily announced that its last scheduled passenger flight would be on 31 May, BA exploited the exclusive value of its unique supersonic aircraft to the last. It ensured that its Concorde flights were packed over the next six months. With all 100 seats filled with paying passengers on most flights it is estimated that BA earned £50m in revenue over this period.

BA's last Concorde departure from Barbados' Grantley Adams International Airport was on 30 August 2003. The airline conducted a mini-North American farewell tour in October 2003 with visits to Toronto, Boston and Washington.

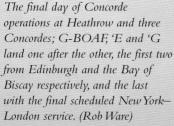

The final day of Concorde operations at Heathrow and three Concordes; G-BOAF, 'E and 'G land one after the other, the first two from Edinburgh and the Bay of Biscay respectively, and the last with the final scheduled New York– London service. (Rob Ware)

All of the five BA Concordes that had received post-Gonesse modifications gradually left Heathrow on loan to aviation museums and the final departure was G-BOAF on 26 November 2003 en route for its birthplace at Filton. (Rob Ware)

UK Tour

For the final week of Concorde operations BA staged a supersonic five-day tour of the UK, giving all regions an opportunity to bid farewell to a much-loved icon. On each day of the tour a different airport was selected for one last visit with a return flight out and back into Heathrow, from, successively Birmingham, Manchester, Cardiff, Belfast and Edinburgh. The tour had been promoted by BA during the summer with the launch of the National Concorde Competition, which gave 650 members of the public and 350 special guests one last chance of a flight.

The last day

British Airways retired its aircraft on 24 October. G-BOAG left New York to a fanfare similar to that enjoyed by Air France's final

Concordes. At the same time, two other aircraft made round trips. G-BOAF flew over the Bay of Biscay carrying VIP guests including many former Concorde pilots, while G-BOAE visited Edinburgh making a supersonic dash up the North Sea.

The airline staged a memorable finale to 27 years of Concorde operations with a piece of theatre at Heathrow when three aircraft landed in quick succession watched by huge crowds. The two round-trip Concordes landed at 16:01 hrs and 16:03 followed at 16:05 hrs by the New York service which had been hosted by BA Chairman Lord Marshall and captained by Concorde chief pilot Mike Bannister. All three aircraft then spent 45 min taxiing around the airport before finally disembarking the last supersonic fare-paying passengers. Among them were Sir David Frost, Joan Collins, Jeremy Clarkson, Nigel Havers, Lord Saatchi, Formula One boss Bernie Ecclestone, Tony Benn and the chairman and CEOs of major concerns including BAE Systems, successor to Concorde builder British Aircraft Corporation.

Final destinations

Both airlines had already announced that their entire Concorde fleets would either be loaned (in BA's case) or donated (by Air France) to aviation museums. The Air France Concordes had already been retired by the time BA services had ceased. The first to leave was F-BVFB, which was delivered after a flight over the Atlantic to Karlsruhe-Baden-Baden Airport where it was dismantled and then moved by barge to the Sinsheim Auto and Technik Museum for display alongside a Tupolev Tu-144. F-BVFA was delivered on 12 June 2003, flying a complement of invited guests to Washington Dulles Airport for display in the Smithsonian Air and Space Museum alongside such aviation icons as the prototype Boeing 707. This Concorde had flown Air France's premier supersonic service more than 27 years, having operated to Dakar on 18 December 1975.

On 14 June, following a round trip over the Bay of Biscay, F-BTSD made a very short hop from Paris-CDG to Paris-Le Bourget for presentation to the *Musée de l'Air*. On 27 June the last Air France Concorde flight saw F-BVFC arriving at Toulouse for preservation by Airbus. The remaining French Concorde, F-BVFF, which had not flown since the Gonesse accident, remained at Paris-Charles de Gaulle for display.

Following the end of services, the first British Concorde to leave Heathrow was G-BOAC. On 31 October it arrived at the Manchester Airport Museum where it is now on display together with an Avro RJX, BAC One-Eleven and Hawker Siddeley Trident.

The most distant final destination for a Concorde was the Boeing Museum of Flight in Seattle. G-BOAG flew there in two stages, first to New York on 3 November and then onwards, flying supersonic by special dispensation, over Canada in 3 hrs 55 mins 12 secs to a tumultuous welcome on 5 November at Seattle. The museum, which already possessed the prototype Boeing 727 and 747, plus a de Havilland Comet 4C, now has an example of the world's only successful supersonic airliner.

Just a week later G-BOAD left for JFK and eventual display at the *Intrepid* Air and Space Museum. BA had flown a weekly service to Barbados from 1994 until 2003 and offered G-BOAE to Grantley Adams Airport in Barbados. On 17 November the penultimate Concorde departure from Heathrow saw 'AE take off for the Caribbean carrying 70 members of BA Concorde staff.

The final flight

The final Concorde Heathrow departure and the last-ever Concorde flight came on 26 November 2003. G-BOAF, appropriately the last aircraft off the Concorde production line, having made its maiden flight on 20 April 1979, flew back to its birthplace at Filton for preservation. Departing Heathrow at 11:30 hr, it made a last brief supersonic dash, carrying 100 BA flight crew over the Bay of Biscay. It then flew a 'lap of honour' above Bristol, passing over Portishead, Clevedon, Weston-super-Mare, Bristol International Airport and Clifton Suspension Bridge, before Concorde flight training manager Captain Les Brodie landed it at Filton soon after 13:00 hrs. The aircraft was greeted by huge crowds which included employees from Rolls-Royce's Patchway factory and the Airbus (former BAC) factory at Filton. Prince Andrew formally accepted it from Capt. Mike Bannister. It had flown a total of 18,257 hrs and is to be the star exhibit in the proposed Bristol Aviation Heritage Museum.

Of BA's seven-strong Concorde fleet two, G-BOAA and G-BOAB, were never modified and were therefore unable to leave by air. G-BOAB remains at Heathrow, while G-BOAA was dismantled in March 2004 and taken by road and then barge down the Thames and up the North Sea to be reassembled at the National Museum of Flight, East Fortune, Scotland.

Conclusion

From the first successful powered flight by the Wright Brothers at Kittyhawk in 1903 there has been an incredible advance in the sophistication of the flying machine. It was, however, a sad irony that in 2003, the centenary year of this achievement, Concorde was grounded. It had proved not only that a supersonic airliner was feasible but also that it could serve for 27 years in airline service. It could well have gone on for much longer, possibly until 2015.

Following the end of commercial supersonic airline operations air transport returned to the humdrum reality of subsonic travel by airliners which appear to be clones of each other. Concorde, though, remains a great engineering achievement and an inspiring icon, while supersonic flight becomes once again the province of military pilots in 'G' suits strapped into ejector seats.

Left: G-BOAF made a brief supersonic flight and then landed at Filton – the final Concorde arrival and the end of supersonic civil flying for the time being. (Phil Jones)

Right: The pilots of G-BOAF, Les Brodie and Mike Bannister, BA's Concorde Fleet Manager, entering into the spirit of the event as Concorde taxies in at Filton. (Phil Jones)

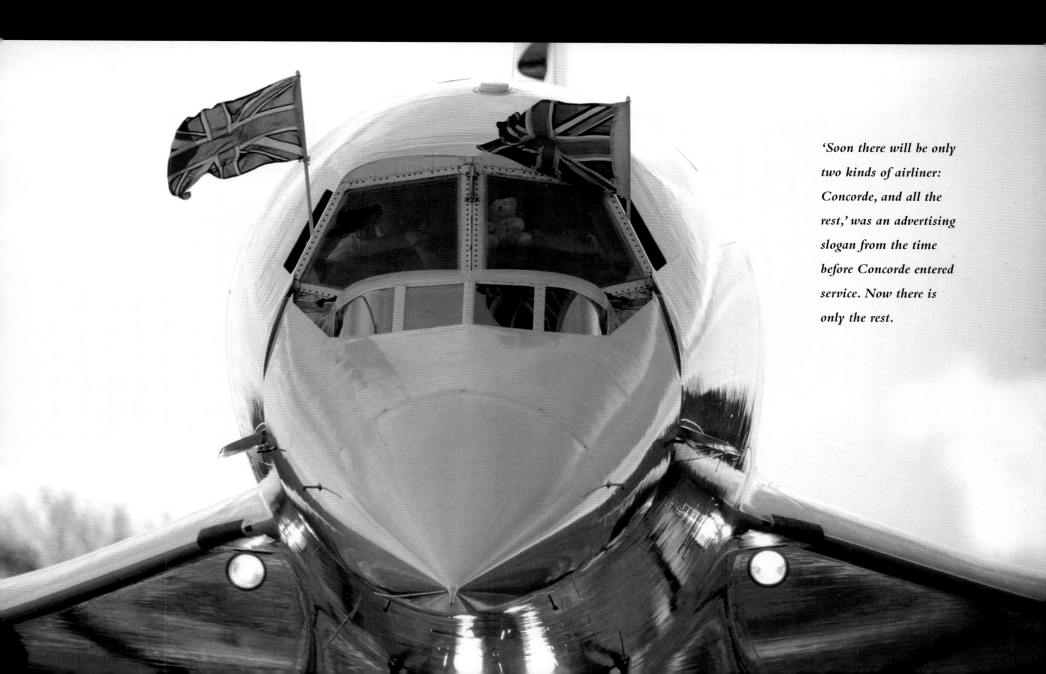

'Soon there will be only two kinds of airliner: Concorde, and all the rest,' was an advertising slogan from the time before Concorde entered service. Now there is only the rest.

Concorde 001. The first prototype, registered F-WTSS, preserved (together with F-BTSD) at the Musée de l'Air at Le Bourget Airport, Paris.

The Concorde Fleet

MSN	Final registration	Built	Operator	History
001	F-WTSS	Toulouse	Aérospatiale	First prototype. First flight 2 March 1969. First supersonic flight 1 October 1969. Flew at Mach 2 on 4 November 1970. Last flight 19 October 1973 from Toulouse to Musée de l'Air et l'Espace, Le Bourget, Paris. Total time 812 hrs.
002	G-BSST	Filton	BAC	Second prototype. First flight 9 April 1969. First supersonic flight 25 March 1970. Flew at Mach 2 on 12 November 1970. Last flight 4 March 1976 Fairford–Fleet Air Arm Museum, Yeovilton, Somerset. Total time 836 hrs.
101	G-AXDN	Filton	BAC	First pre-production prototype. First flight 17 December 1971. Flew at Mach 2.23 on 8 April 1974 to become fastest Concorde. Last flight 20 August 1977 Filton–Imperial War Museum, Duxford, Cambridgeshire. Total time 633 hrs.
102	F-WTSA	Toulouse	Aérospatiale	Second pre-production prototype. First flight 10 January 1973. Last flight 20 May 1976 Toulouse–Paris Orly Airport. Now preserved Musée Delta, Orly Airport, Paris. Total time 657 hrs.
201	F-WTSB	Toulouse	Aérospatiale	First production prototype. First flight 6 December 1973. Last flight 19 April 1985 Chateauroux–Airbus Toulouse for preservation. Total time 910 hrs.
202	G-BBDG	Filton	BAC	Second production prototype. First flight 13 February 1974. Last flight 24 December 1981. Stored at Filton and used as spares source for BA. Dismantled and delivered by road May/June 2004 to Brooklands Museum, Weybridge, Surrey. Total time 1,435 hrs.
203	F-BTSC	Toulouse	Air France	First flight, as F-WTSC, on 31 January 1975. Leased Air France 6 January 1976–8 December 1976 then returned to Aérospatiale. Leased by Aérospatiale for use in film Airport '80: The Concorde 1978/9. Leased to Air France 11 June 1979; purchased by Air France 23 October 1980. Crashed Gonesse 25 July 2000. Total time 11,989 hrs.
204	G-BOAC	Filton	British Airways	First flight 27 February 1975. Delivered to BA 13 February 1976. Registered as G-N81AC/N81AC by British Airways/Braniff Airways 5 January 1979; reverted to G-BOAC for BA 11 August 1980. Last flight 31 October 2003 Heathrow–Aviation Viewing Park, Manchester Airport. Total time 22,260 hrs.
205	F-BVFA	Toulouse	Air France	First flight 25 October 1975. Delivered to Air France 19 December 1975. Last flight 12 June 2003 CDG–Washington Dulles. Now on display at Smithsonian Museum's Udvar-Hazy Center Washington Dulles Airport, USA. Total time 17,824 hrs.
206	G-BOAA	Filton	British Airways	First flight 5 November 1975. Delivered to BA 14 January 1976. January 1979 registered as G-N94AA/N94AA by British Airways/Braniff Airways; re-registered as G-BOAA by BA 28 July 1980. Last flight 12 August 2000; did not fly again as not modified following Gonesse accident. Dismantled April 2004 and delivered by surface transport to Museum of Flight, East Fortune, Scotland. Total time 22,769 hrs.
207	F-BVFB	Toulouse	Air France	First flight 6 March 1976. Delivered to Air France 8 April 1976. Re-registered as N94FB by Air France/Braniff Airways 12 January 1979; reverted to F-BVFB by Air France 1 June 1980. Last flight to Karlsrühe-Baden-Baden 24 June 2003. Dismantled and delivered by road and river to the Auto and Technik Museum, Sinsheim, Germany. Total time 14,771 hrs.
208	G-BOAB	Filton	British Airways	First flight 18 May 1976. Delivered to BA 30 September 1976. Registered as G-N94AB/N94AB by British Airways/Braniff Airways 12 January 1979; re-registered as G-BOAB by BA 17 September 1980. Last flight 15 August 2000; did not fly again as not modified following Gonesse accident. Preserved London Heathrow Airport. Total time 22,296 hrs.

MSN	Final registration	Built	Operator	History
209	F-BVFC	Toulouse	Air France	First flight 9 July 1976. Delivered to Air France 13 August 1976. 12 January 1979 re-registered as N94FC by Air France/Braniff Airways 12 January 1979; re-registered as F-BVFC by Air France 1 June 1980. Last flight 27 June 2003 Paris CDG-Airbus Toulouse. Total time 14,322 hrs.
210	G-BOAD	Filton	British Airways	First flight 25 August 1976. Delivered to BA 6 December 1976. Re-registered as G-N94AD/N94AD by British Airways/Braniff Airways 5 January 1979; Singapore Airlines livery applied to left-hand side during 1979/80; re-registered as G-BOAD by BA 19 June 1980. Last flight 10 November 2003 Heathrow–JFK New York. Transferred by barge to Intrepid Sea, Air and Space Museum, New York, USA. Total time 23,397 hrs.
211	F-BVFD	Toulouse	Air France	First flight 10 February 1977. Delivered to Air France 26 March 1977. Registered as N94FD by Air France/Braniff Airways 12 January 1979; re-registered as F-BVFD by Air France 1 June 1980. Damaged in heavy landing Dakar November 1977. Last flight 25 July 1982. Withdrawn from use March 1991 and scrapped December 1994. Total time 5,814 hrs.
212	G-BOAE	Filton	British Airways	First flight 17 March 1977. Delivered to BA 20 July 1977. 5 January 1979 re-registered as G-N94AE/N94AE by British Airways/Braniff Airways. 1 July 1980 re-registered as G-BOAE by BA. Last flight 17 November 2003 Heathrow–Grantley Adams Airport, Bridgetown, Barbados. Total time 23,376 hrs.
213	F-BTSD	Toulouse	Air France	First flight as F-WJAM 26 June 1978. Delivered to Air France 18 September 1978. Registered as F-BTSD and returned to Aérospatiale 12 March 1979. Purchased by Air France 23 October 1980. Pepsi livery applied April 1996. Holds records for fastest global circumnavigation in easterly and westerly directions. Last flight 14 June 2003 Paris CDG–Musée de l'Air et l'Espace, Le Bourget, Paris. Total time 12,974 hrs.
214	G-BOAG	Filton	British Airways	First flight as G-BFKW 21 April 1978 registered to British Aerospace. Delivered to British Airways 6 February 1980. Re-registered as G-BOAG 9 February 1981. Last flight 3 November 2003 Heathrow–JFK New York. Flew supersonically over Canada to Museum of Flight Seattle USA, 5 November 2003. Total time 16,239 hrs.
215	F-BVFF	Toulouse	Air France	First flight as F-WJAN 26 December 1978. Delivered to Air France 23 October 1980 registered as F-BVFF. Did not fly after July 2000 as not modified following Gonesse accident. Preserved Charles De Gaulle Airport, Paris. Total time 12,421 hrs.
216	G-BOAF	Filton	British Airways	Last Concorde built. First flight as G-BFKX 20 April 1979 registered to British Aerospace. Re-registered as G-N94AF/G-BOAF 14 December 1979. Delivered to British Airways 9 June 1980; re-registered as G-BOAF by BA 12 June 1980. Made the final Concorde flight Heathrow–Bristol Aero Collection, Filton, Bristol 26 November 2003. Total time 18,257 hrs.

Concorde production statistics:

Prototypes:	2
Pre-production prototypes:	2
Production prototypes:	2
Production:	14

Production sites: Filton and Toulouse,
which each built 10 Concordes and one
test specimen

Total Number completed : 20 & 2 test specimens

Concorde 002*. The second Concorde prototype and first British example G-BSST at the Fleet Air Arm Museum at Yeovilton. G-BSST flew for almost six years before retirement to Yeovilton. On the left of the photograph is the blue tail of the BAC 221 which was used as a research tool for Concorde. (Author's collection)*

Concorde 101*. G-AXDN has been at the Imperial War Museum at Duxford since it was flown there by Brian Trubshaw and John Cochrane on 20 August 1977. It is now preserved in the huge AirSpace hangar but is seen here outside on 9 September 2005. (Jean-Pierre Touzeau)*

Concorde 102*. F-WTSA was the second pre-production prototype that at one time originally carried BA colours on one side and Air France's on the other. This is how it looked on 11 October 2008 at the Musée Delta, Orly Airport, Paris. (Jean-Pierre Touzeau)*

Concorde 201. The first production prototype F-WTSB is preserved at the Airbus factory at Toulouse. It first flew from there on 6 December 1973 and returned there on 19 April 1985 for preservation. (Pedro Aragao)

Concorde 202. Following its last flight on 24 December 1981 G-BBDG languished at Filton and was then purchased by BA for spares use. With the end of Concorde operations it was loaned to the Brooklands Museum and taken there by road for reassembly in May–June 2004, where it has been repainted in the BA livery in which it first flew. (Author)

Concorde 203. F-BTSC, the first production standard Concorde was written off at Gonesse on 25 July 2000, killing all on board. It is seen here landing at Dublin on 7 November 1997. (Carl Ford)

Concorde 204. G-BOAC, the flagship of BA's Concorde fleet, arriving for preservation at Manchester Airport on 31 October 2003. (Phil Jones)

Concorde 205. *F-BVFA now preserved at the Smithsonian Museum's Udvar-Hazy Center Washington-Dulles Airport. (Pawel Kierzkowski)*

Concorde 206. *Only five of BA's seven Concordes were modified after the Paris accident leaving two which could not be flown out of Heathrow to preservation. Thus G-BOAA had to be dismantled and transported by barge down the Thames passing the House of Commons on its way to the North Sea and the Museum of Flight at East Fortune near Edinburgh. (Vin Man)*

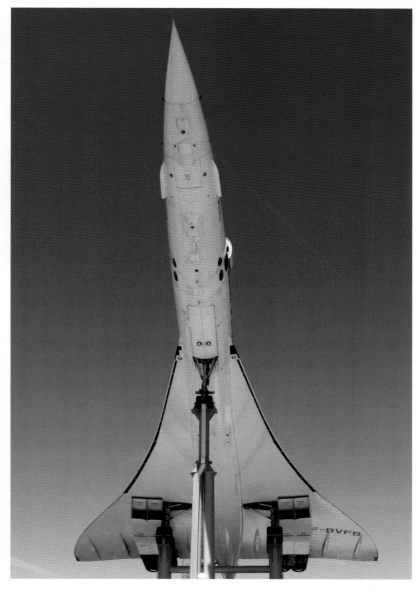

Concorde 207. *F-BVFB made its last flight from Paris Charles de Gaulle Airport to Karlsrühe-Baden-Baden on 24 June 2003 and was dismantled and reassembled at the Auto & Technik Museum, Sinsheim, Germany. A Tupolev Tu-144 is also preserved at Sinsheim. (Fabian Rausch)*

Concorde 209. *F-BVFC preserved at Airbus Toulouse together with a French Air Force Armstrong Whitworth Meteor NF11, a sister aircraft to the Meteor used as a chase aircraft for the prototype Concorde's early test flights. André Turcat, who made Concorde's maiden flight in 1969, was on board F-BVFC during its final flight on 27 June 2003 to Toulouse, where the French Concordes were assembled. (Jean-Pierre Touzeau)*

Concorde 208. *G-BOAB was the second BA Concorde not modified after the Gonesse accident and did not fly after August 2000. It is preserved by British Airways at Heathrow Airport. (Paul Robinson)*

Concorde 210. *G-BOAD on a barge adjacent to the Intrepid Sea, Air and Space Museum which is based on the World War Two US aircraft carrier USS 'Intrepid' in New York. The Concorde is now situated on the dockside adjacent to the Carrier. (Marco Louwe)*

Concorde 211. *F-BVFD was unique amongst all Concordes as it was withdrawn from use and scrapped at Paris-Charles de Gaulle in 1994. (Michel Gilliand)*

Concorde 212. Barbados was one of BA's regular Concorde destinations and to mark the significance of this on 17 November 2003 G-BOAE flew to Barbados for preservation. (Barbados Concorde Experience)

Concorde 213. Air France's F-BTSD is now preserved alongside the first prototype F-WTSS at the Musée de l'Air at Le Bourget Airport, Paris. (Jean-Pierre Touzeau)

Concorde 214. G-BOAG making its final landing at Boeing Field, Seattle on 5 November 2003, for preservation at the Museum of Flight after a supersonic flight across the Atlantic via New York and then over Canada. (Ben Wang)

Concorde 215. Of Air France's five Concordes surviving at the time of the cessation of services in 2003 only F-BVFF remained unmodified following the accident in July 2000 and did not fly again. It is now dramatically perched at Charles de Gaulle Airport, Paris. (Jean-Pierre Touzeau)

Concorde 216. *The last Concorde built, G-BOAF, on display at Filton where it was built. This Concorde made the final flight of a Concorde on 26 November 2003 from Heathrow to Filton.*
(Anthony Best)

APPENDIX 2

Concorde Data

	Concorde Prototypes	Concorde Pre-production prototypes	Concorde Production
Length	184 ft 6 in	193 ft 0 in / 203 ft 9 in	203 ft 9 in
Wingspan	83 ft 10 in	83 ft 10 in	83 ft 10 in
Height	36 ft 6 in	38 ft	40 ft 1 in
MTOW	326,000 lb	350,000 lb	412,000 lb
Max cruise speed	Mach 2	Mach 2	Mach 2
Take-off speed	225 mph	225 mph	246 mph
Landing speed	186 mph	186 mph	186 mph
Payload range	n.a.	n.a.	3,870 miles
Passengers	n.a.	n.a.	100
Rolls-Royce Olympus	32,825 lbs	32,520 lbs	32,520 lbs
Olympus with reheat	34,370 lbs	35,080 lbs	35,080 lbs

APPENDIX 3

Concorde Chronology

1950	6 May	First run of an Olympus engine in a ground test bed
1955	29 August	Olympus-Canberra WD952 wins world altitude record of 65,876 ft
1956	5 November	British Supersonic Transport Aircraft Committee first meeting
1962	29 November	Signing of the Treaty between Britain and France to develop Concorde
1963	May	Options placed by Pan Am, BOAC and Air France
1966	9 September	First flight of Vulcan XA903 with Olympus 593
1967	11 December	Roll-out of French prototype 001 F-WTSS
1968	31 December	First flight of the Soviet SST, Tupolev Tu-144
	19 September	Roll-out of British prototype 002 G-BSST
1969	2 March	Maiden flight of 001 F-WTSS
	9 April	Maiden flight of 002 G-BSST
	1 October	F-WTSS exceeds Mach 1
1970	4 November	F-WTSS exceeds Mach 2
1971	17 December	Maiden flight of 01 G-AXDN
1972		Total of 79 options for Concorde from 18 airlines
1973	10 January	Maiden flight of 02 F-WTSA
1975	5 December	Concorde certified
1976	21 January	First Services by BA (London–Bahrain) and Air France (Paris–Dakar)
1976	24 May	BA & Air France services to Washington begin
1977	22 November	BA & Air France services to New York begin
1979	20 April	Final Concorde built makes its supersonic maiden flight from Filton, registered G-BFKX (later G-BOAF)

1984	March	BA and Air France take on financial responsibility for their fleets' aircraft and spares from the respective Governments
1996	7 February	Fastest flight from JFK to Heathrow in 2 hrs 52 mins and 50 secs
2000	25 July	F-BTSC crashes near Charles de Gaulle airport.
	16 August	Certification withdrawn
2001	5 September	Concorde re-certified
	7 November	BA and Air France services to New York resume
2003	10 April	BA and Air France announce withdrawal of Concorde from service
	31 May	Final Air France service (New York–Paris)
	27 June	Final Air France Concorde flight (F-BVFC CDG–Toulouse)
	24 October	Final BA service (New York–London)
	26 November	Final Concorde flight (G-BOAF Heathrow–Filton)

BIBLIOGRAPHY

Books
Aérospatiale: 1970–1990 20th Anniversary, Gerard Maoui, Le Cherche-Midi Editeur
British Aircraft Corporation, Charles Gardner, Batsford 1981
Caravelle: the Complete Story, John Wegg, Airways 2005
Concorde, Brian Trubshaw, Sutton 2002
Concorde: the inside story, Geoffrey Knight, Weidenfeld & Nicholson 1976
Concorde: Story of a Supersonic Pioneer, Kenneth Owen, Science Museum 2001
From Bouncing Bomb to Concorde, Richard Gardner, Sutton 2006
Olympus: The Inside Story, Alan Baxter, Rolls-Royce Heritage Trust 2007
Prelude to Concorde HP 115, Henry Matthews & Peter Davison, HPM Publications 2005
Sound Barrier, Peter Caygill, Pen & Sword 2006
A Span of Wings, Archibald Russell, Airlife 1992
Test Pilot, Brian Trubshaw, Sutton 1998

Accident reports
Report on the accident to British Aircraft Corporation/SNIAS Concorde 102, G-BOAB, over the North Atlantic, on 21 March 1992. CAA 1992
Accident on 25 July 2000 at La Patte d'Oie in Gonesse to the Concorde registered F-BTSC operated by Air France. BEA *(Bureau D'Enquetes D'Analyses pour la Sécurité D'Aviation Civile)* 2002

Magazines & other publications
Aeroplane
Aircraft Engineering
Air International
Air Pictorial
Flight International
Interavia
Manufacturers' brochures